T0215530

Cloud-Native Microservices with Apache Pulsar

Build Distributed Messaging Microservices

Rahul Sharma
Mohammad Atyab

Apress®

Cloud-Native Microservices with Apache Pulsar: Build Distributed Messaging Microservices

Rahul Sharma
Delhi, Delhi, India

Mohammad Atyab
New Delhi, India

ISBN-13 (pbk): 978-1-4842-7838-3
https://doi.org/10.1007/978-1-4842-7839-0

ISBN-13 (electronic): 978-1-4842-7839-0

Copyright © 2022 by Rahul Sharma and Mohammad Atyab

This work is subject to copyright. All rights are reserved by the Publisher, whether the whole or part of the material is concerned, specifically the rights of translation, reprinting, reuse of illustrations, recitation, broadcasting, reproduction on microfilms or in any other physical way, and transmission or information storage and retrieval, electronic adaptation, computer software, or by similar or dissimilar methodology now known or hereafter developed.

Trademarked names, logos, and images may appear in this book. Rather than use a trademark symbol with every occurrence of a trademarked name, logo, or image we use the names, logos, and images only in an editorial fashion and to the benefit of the trademark owner, with no intention of infringement of the trademark.

The use in this publication of trade names, trademarks, service marks, and similar terms, even if they are not identified as such, is not to be taken as an expression of opinion as to whether or not they are subject to proprietary rights.

While the advice and information in this book are believed to be true and accurate at the date of publication, neither the authors nor the editors nor the publisher can accept any legal responsibility for any errors or omissions that may be made. The publisher makes no warranty, express or implied, with respect to the material contained herein.

Managing Director, Apress Media LLC: Welmoed Spahr
Acquisitions Editor: Celestin Suresh John
Development Editor: James Markham
Coordinating Editor: Shrikant Vishwakarma
Copyeditor: Kim Burton Wiseman

Cover designed by eStudioCalamar

Cover image designed by Pexels

Distributed to the book trade worldwide by Springer Science+Business Media LLC, 1 New York Plaza, Suite 4600, New York, NY 10004. Phone 1-800-SPRINGER, fax (201) 348-4505, e-mail orders-ny@springer-sbm. com, or visit www.springeronline.com. Apress Media, LLC is a California LLC and the sole member (owner) is Springer Science + Business Media Finance Inc (SSBM Finance Inc). SSBM Finance Inc is a **Delaware** corporation.

For information on translations, please e-mail booktranslations@springernature.com; for reprint, paperback, or audio rights, please e-mail bookpermissions@springernature.com, or visit http://www.apress.com/rights-permissions.

Apress titles may be purchased in bulk for academic, corporate, or promotional use. eBook versions and licenses are also available for most titles. For more information, reference our Print and eBook Bulk Sales web page at http://www.apress.com/bulk-sales.

Any source code or other supplementary material referenced by the author in this book is available to readers on GitHub via the book's product page, located at www.apress.com/978-1-4842-7838-3. For more detailed information, please visit http://www.apress.com/source-code.

Printed on acid-free paper

Table of Contents

About the Authors

Rahul Sharma is a software developer with 17 years of experience in Java/J2EE and Python applications. An open source enthusiast, he has contributed to various projects, including Apache Crunch. He has worked extensively with Kubernetes and microservices for companies of various sizes, from enterprises to start-ups.

Mohammad Atyab is a software developer with more than 13 years of developing products. He has worked in various languages, primarily Java/J2EE, Python, and C++. He has a passion for building products and has created web-based scalable applications in chatbots in the ecommerce, marketing, and financial domains. He has worked extensively in big data and artificial intelligence with large enterprises and start-ups.

About the Technical Reviewer

 **Pramiti Guha** is currently working as a Senior System Analyst with IBM. She has 11 years of experience in application development and modernization with organizations like Infosys, Deloitte, and Accenture. She has led teams that delivered application modernization projects for clients in a wide range of domains, including finance, healthcare, telecom, travel, and transportation. She has extensive experience working with programming languages like Java and Python, a variety of distributed messaging systems (Confluent Kafka, Apache Pulsar, Redis, AWS SNS), and open source data storage technologies like MongoDB, Couchbase, and CouchDB. Pramiti is an Open Group Certified Technical Specialist.

Acknowledgments

Many people contributed to the publication of this book. I would like to take this opportunity and express my gratitude to each of them.

My sincerest thanks go to Celestin Suresh John for providing us with this exciting opportunity. Your confidence in the project provided the necessary groundwork.

I would like to thank Shrikant Vishwakarma for getting the project delivered. Since the project's inception, you have been vital to its success. Your editorial support made the project go from strength to strength.

I would like to thank Pramiti Guha and James Markham for their valuable feedback. Your suggestions helped me to deliver our ideas in a better way.

I would like to thank my co-author, Mohammad Atyab, for being incredibly knowledgeable and helpful. Your experience and willingness made the project a success. Thanks to the brainstorming sessions, the ideas were expressed clearly.

Moreover, I wish to express my appreciation to my parents, my loving and supportive wife, Swati, and my children, Rudra and Pranshi. You inspire me and encourage me constantly. Thanks for your patience and listening to my gibberish when not everything went according to plan.

Last but not least, I would like to thank my friends who have provided me with knowledge. I appreciated our discussions on various subjects. They often served as a benchmark for evaluating our knowledge.

—Rahul Sharma

Introduction

Enterprises are adopting containers to replace their legacy applications as part of their digital transformation programs. This strategy results in distributed systems with exceptional flexibility in responding to changing business demands. But building distributed systems requires integrated solutions that can deliver at scale. It has been found that application integration is one of the most critical yet largely concealed requirements of distributed architecture.

According to one Gartner study, integration accounts for about 50% of the time and cost in building modern cloud solutions. Thus, enterprises need next-generation cloud-native integration solutions that are lean, lightweight, secure, fault-tolerant, and can support various integration protocols.

Apache Pulsar is a multitenant, high-performance cloud-native messaging and streaming platform. It offers a large set of out-of-the-box integration options. This book begins by introducing Pulsar's architecture. The first few chapters build a foundation of message-driven architecture and explain the setup of all the required Pulsar components. You explore the transform, filter, and resiliency capabilities available in Pulsar. Security is an important aspect of any application, and this book goes over authentication and authorization. The final chapters cover Pulsar deployment in Kubernetes and deploying microservices.

This book is a comprehensive hands-on guide for those who are new to Apache Pulsar. It is intended for experienced software developers who want to build systems using cloud-native technologies. We do not assume any prior knowledge of Apache Pulsar or any other messaging system. The book is not specific to any programming language, even though all examples are covered using the Pulsar Java client library.

## CHAPTER 1

Introduction to Apache Pulsar

Traditionally, most enterprise applications were developed on monolith architectures. These applications were quick to create at the early stages, but the maintenance and operational teams often encountered many challenges when working on them. Over the last decade, distributed application architecture has become the primary enterprise development strategy. It is well supported by enterprise cloud infrastructure adaption and container adaption plans. As a result, we no longer build simple applications; instead, we typically develop end-to-end platforms. These platforms consist of numerous applications that communicate using lightweight communication protocols, like REST APIs or remote procedure calls (RPC). These platforms cut across organizational boundaries and often require complex tools and architectures to deliver their intended benefits.

Distributed Challenges

Building a complete enterprise platform is more complex than building an application on a particular architecture. A platform should provide flexibility to meet a business's needs while maintaining non-functional aspects like performance, scalability, availability, and resiliency. Thus, it must address the following challenges.

1

© Rahul Sharma and Mohammad Atyab 2022
R. Sharma and M. Atyab, *Cloud-Native Microservices with Apache Pulsar*,
https://doi.org/10.1007/978-1-4842-7839-0_1

Each of these events is likely to trigger one or more actions or processes in response. EDA is also known as *messaging architecture*. It lets you build distributed systems with the following characteristics.

- **Loose coupling**: Coupling is the interdependence among different components of an application. In EDA, an event producer has no dependence on the consumer of an event. The producer is not concerned about where the consumer is deployed or what kind of processing is performed. Similarly, an event consumer has no dependence on a producer, apart from raising the event. Moreover, an event is self-contained; all the required information is unaware of any consequences. The concept of loose coupling offers several benefits, such as application independence and quicker releases.

- **Fault-tolerant**: EDA is often resilient because each component is responsible for its processing without any dependency. Thus, a failed or underloaded application has no impact on the other deployed applications. Moreover, all events are saved and delivered to a consumer when they are available. This means that EDA allows services to be patched independently without any loss of data.

- **Diversity**: EDA offers diversity to enterprise application technologies. Teams can create producers and consumers in different languages, use different libraries, and use different data stores. Each of these components may have the following event delivery requirements.

  - Real time: For user request processing

  - Day/week events: For analytics and reporting

  - Since time: For upgrades and new application deployments

EDA allows you to build each component with the frameworks and tools that are best suited to its needs. Moreover, each component allows different protocols like REST, RPC using protocol buffers, and legacy systems.

- **Standardization**: Since producers are unaware of the associated consumers, they often generate self-contained events. Each consumer gets the same event, a single source of truth, which can be analyzed and processed independently. New consumers can be created in the event's structure to offer new capabilities.

- **Low latency**: Events are associated with the law of diminishing returns. This means that the older an event, the lesser value it is. Thus, it is of utmost impotent to respond to events as quickly as possible. Therefore, all consumers must be notified of the event as close to the same time as possible.

EDA lays the foundation for the continued processing of events. Traditionally, these events were stored in a data warehouse and processed at a later point in time. This suboptimal approach caused unavailable operational data for business-critical demands. Alternatively, EDA can consume, process, and aggregate events in real time to enable novel solutions to business challenges. Organizations reap the following benefits of EDA adaption.

Innovation

EDA promotes independent components developed by teams providing a service. These teams have ownership of their data and services. They can adopt frameworks, tools, and practices to deliver their requirements. They are not blocked by early technology choices, which are difficult to reverse. This results in an autonomous engineering culture within the organization.

Moreover, development teams are usually well aware of the shortcomings of their services. These issues can be addressed using autonomous decision-making capabilities that can frequently fix problems and improve service quality. Here again, teams are fully empowered to select the appropriate tools and frameworks, which ultimately leads to the improved technical quality of the overall product.

Resilience

Fault isolation is the act of limiting the impact of a failure to a limited subsystem/component. This principle allows a subsystem to fail as long as it does not impact the complete application. The distributed nature of EDA offers fault isolation, a principal requirement of building resilient systems. Any component that is experiencing failures can be handled independently. Developers can fix issues and deploy new versions while the rest of the application continues to function independently.

Resilience, or fault tolerance, is often defined as an application's ability to function correctly in the event of some part's failure. EDA integrates decoupled components with asynchronous communications, thereby proving a solution to SLA inversion.

> SLA *inversion is when a system must provide high availability but depends on systems of lower availability.*
>
> —Michael Nygard, author of *Release It!*

A synchronous system's SLA is the product of all the SLAs of the dependent services. On the other hand, services can provide their independent levels of SLA if built using decoupled middleware.

Scalability

Scalability is defined as the capability of a system to handle the growth of work. But, application load does not increase uniformly across all subsystems. It is often the case that some parts of the system get more traffic than others. The decoupling offered by EDA enables the organization to understand the volume supported by each component. Developers can adopt appropriate task parallelization or clustering techniques for each service to enhance the system throughput. They can adopt relevant programming languages and frameworks, fine-tuned with the best possible configuration.

On the other hand, EDA offers rate limiting and throttling capabilities to control event flow until idle consumers are available. They offer out-of-box configurations to support varied needs, from a single instance of legacy application to multiple instances of stateless consumers.

Extensible

EDA supports the integration of diverse protocols and data formats by providing pluggable connectors. It can also provide support for propriety protocols by developing producers and consumers for propriety data exchange. This extensibility lets you build solutions by adding more components for changing requirements rather than enhancing one component. This divide-and-conquer approach improves overall system performance while promoting orthogonal thinking.

EDA can help organizations achieve a flexible system that adapts to changes and make quick decisions. These decisions can be implemented quickly with components that are developed, deployed, and scaled independently. These systems can consume, process, aggregate, or correlate extremely large events or information in real time. Developers can easily extend and enhance these systems by using open source solutions.

EDA requires an event integration platform with low operating costs. The platform should run on commodity hardware with minimal CPU, memory, and storage resource usage. It should be scalable on cloud platforms to support enterprise-wide applications built using containers.

The next section introduces Apache Pulsar, a cloud-native integration platform.

Apache Pulsar

Apache Pulsar is a distributed, open source, event-streaming platform created by Yahoo!. In 2016, Yahoo! donated Pulsar to the Apache Software Foundation. Pulsar has progressively developed and matured under their open source guidance.

Historically, Yahoo! was looking for a solution to integrate its products deployed across the globe. In addition to integration demands, the solution was expected to provide the following.

- Multi-tenancy

- Geo-replication

- Durability guarantees

Existing solutions had several challenges with supporting these features. Thus, Pulsar was envisioned to integrate various services developed and deployed at scale. Let's briefly discuss some of the salient features offered by Apache Pulsar.

Unified Messaging Model

Event processing evolved from message-oriented middleware, which had the following two models of execution.

- **Point-to-point** is a queue-based system in which a message is delivered to one consumer at a time.

- It enables each layer to scale independently, thereby providing elastic capacity.

- By leveraging the ability of adaptable environments (such as the cloud and containers) to automatically scale resources up and down, it can dynamically adapt to traffic spikes.

- It improves system availability and manageability by significantly reducing the complexity of cluster expansions and upgrades.

- It is container-friendly and cloud native.

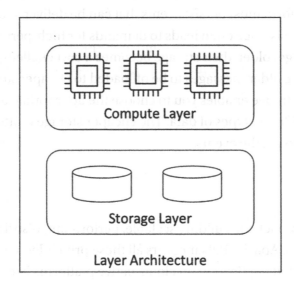

Figure 1-2. Layer architecture

Figure 1-2 shows the compute and storage layers of a Pulsar cluster.

The next section looks at how these layers provide scalability and availability characteristics to Apache Pulsar.

Brokers

The compute layer in Apache Pulsar consists of a set of brokers that receive and deliver messages. The compute layer is "stateless" because it doesn't persist any messages locally. This allows Pulsar to deploy more brokers (see Figure 1-3), when there is surge in traffic. Moreover any broker can take over from another failed broker. Pulsar performs automatic load balancing of all brokers. It monitors all brokers' CPU, memory, and network usage and dynamically distributes topics between them.

Each topic is assigned to one of the available brokers, known as the owner broker of the topic. Pulsar producers and consumers connect to the owner broker to send and receive events from the owner broker. If the owner broker dies, another takes its place to ensure availability.

Bookies

The persistence layer in Apache Pulsar comprises a set of Apache BookKeeper nodes. BookKeeper stores data in for logs across a cluster of nodes. Each BookKeeper node is called a *bookie*.

A topic is divided into multiple smaller segments, which are distributed across different bookies. The segmentation results in performance, scalability, and availability of events data. Since the data associated with a given topic is not tied to a specific storage node, it is easier to replace or scale nodes. The design also mitigates storage or bandwidth bottleneck challenges often imposed by the smallest or slowest node.

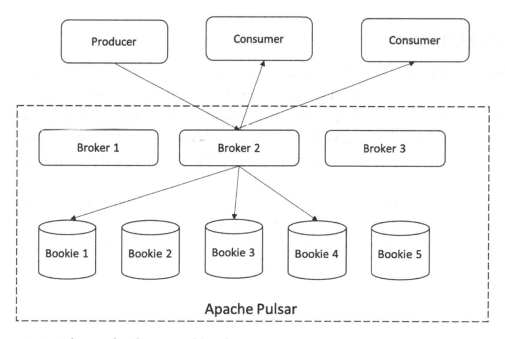

Figure 1-3. *Clients, brokers, and bookies*

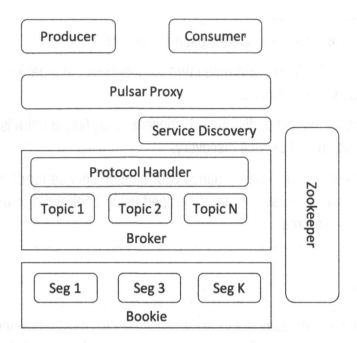

Figure 1-4. *Pulsar components*

Figure 1-4 shows the components required for working with Pulsar. The next section looks at the different kinds of installations provided by Pulsar.

Pulsar Setup

Pulsar is released often. Binary artifacts for all releases are available on the Apache Pulsar download page. The product is released for nix architecture. When writing this book, Pulsar 2.8.1 was the latest release (see Figure 1-5).

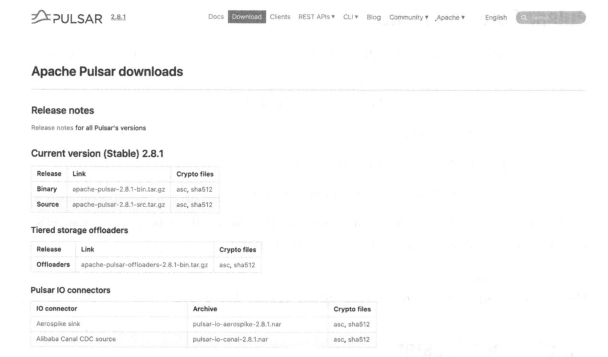

Figure 1-5. *Apache Pulsar release*

The remaining part of this chapter demonstrates the installation of Pulsar 2.8.1. You can download the appropriate release using any of the following methods.

- Open `https://pulsar.apache.org/en/download/` page and click the release: apache-pulsar-2.8.1-bin.tar.gz.

- Execute the curl command for the terminal: curl -o `https://www.apache.org/dyn/mirrors/mirrors.cgi?action=download&filenam e=pulsar/pulsar-2.8.1/apache-pulsar-2.8.1-bin.tar.gz`.

- Unpack the archive: tar -zxvf apache-pulsar-2.8.1-bin.tar.gz. The unarchived distribution contains bin, conf, example, licenses, and lib folders.

```
apachepulsar/pulsar:2.8.1 \
bin/pulsar standalone
```

Multi-Node Cluster

Pulsar can be deployed for enterprise-scale production environments in large clusters. The process involves deploying each of the following components.

1. Prepare ZooKeeper.

2. Add bookies.

3. Add brokers.

A multi-node deployment needs many nodes, for bookies and brokers. Next, let's create a lean cluster by using only two nodes.

ZooKeeper

ZooKeeper is essential to Pulsar. It provides configuration management service discovery capabilities. First, you must deploy a ZooKeeper instance to one node.

1. Add the following server address to `conf/Zookeeper.conf`.

    ```
    server.1=192.16.1.5:2888:3888
    ```

2. Zookeeper is configured to write to the data/zookeeper location. You must add the server ID to the myid file under this location.

    ```
    echo 1 > data/zookeeper/myid
    ```

3. You can interactively start ZooKeeper using the following command.

    ```
    $ bin/pulsar zookeeper
    ```

Next, you need to add the Pulsar cluster configuration to ZooKeeper using the following command.

```
$ bin/pulsar initialize-cluster-metadata --cluster pulsar-cluster-1
--zookeeper 192.16.1.5:2181 --configuration-store 192.16.1.5:2181  --
web-service-url http://192.16.1.4:8080 --web-service-url-tls
https://192.16.1.4:8443 --broker-service-url pulsar://192.16.1.4:6650
--broker-service-url-tls pulsar+ssl://192.16.1.4:6651
```

This configuration does the following.

- Specifies the cluster name as pulsar-cluster-1

- Provides the first node address for the location of ZooKeeper and the configuration store

- Provides a second node address for the location of the Pulsar cluster

- Provides a third node address for the location of broker cluster

Bookies

Next, you must create a bookie cluster. This is done by starting the bookie with the ZooKeeper location. You must update the location in conf/bookkeeper.conf.

```
zkServers=192.16.1.5:2181
```

Interactively start the bookie using the following command.

```
$ bin/pulsar bookie
```

Pulsar packages the BookKeeper shell for debugging and troubleshooting issues with bookies. You can use it to validate if the bookie is working fine using the following command.

```
$ bin/bookkeeper shell bookiesanity
```

Brokers

Finally, you must create a single-node broker cluster. To do this, update conf/broker.conf with the following configuration.

```
zookeeperServers=192.16.1.5:2181
configurationStoreServers=192.16.1.5:2181
clusterName=pulsar-cluster-1
brokerServicePort=6650
brokerServicePortTls=6651
webServicePort=8080
webServicePortTls=8443
managedLedgerDefaultEnsembleSize=1
managedLedgerDefaultWriteQuorum=1
managedLedgerDefaultAckQuorum=1
```

This configuration does the following.

- Provides a node address for the location of ZooKeeper and the configuration store

- Specifies the cluster name as pulsar-cluster-1

- Provides port information for the Pulsar cluster

- Provides port information for the broker

There is one bookie in the cluster so you must update

`managedLedgerDefaultEnsembleSize`, `managedLedgerDefaultWriteQuorum` and `managedLedgerDefaultAckQuorum` to skip replication.

After updating, interactively start the broker using the following command.

```
$ bin/pulsar broker
```

You can look up clusters and brokers by using the pulsar-admin command.

```
$ bin/pulsar-admin clusters list
"pulsar-cluster-1"

$ bin/pulsar-admin brokers list pulsar-cluster-1
"192.168.1.4:8080"
```

Verify Cluster

You can connect to Pulsar using its clients. Chapter 2 works with Pulsar language-specific libraries to build custom solutions. But as part of cluster tools, Pulsar comes packaged with command-line clients that validate a cluster. Each of these clients must determine the locations for Pulsar clusters and brokers. This is provided by updating conf/client.conf with the following details.

```
webServiceUrl=http://192.168.1.4:8080/
brokerServiceUrl=pulsar://192.168.1.4:6650/
```

After updating the locations, you can start a console message output consumer using the following command.

```
$ bin/pulsar-client consume   persistent://public/default/test   -n 10   -s
"consumer-test"   -t "Exclusive"
```

This command configures the consumer as follows.

1. Listens on the public/default/test topic

2. Waits to read ten messages specified by the -n flag

3. Creates an exclusive subscription specified by the -t flag

4. Names the subscription consumer-test

Next, you must create a producer using the following command.

```
bin/pulsar-client produce   persistent://public/default/test   -n 10   -m
"Created My First cluster"
```

This command configures the consumer as follows.

1. Publishes to the public/default/test topic

2. Replicates the message ten times, specified by the -n flag

3. Sends a Created My First Cluster message

You can verify that the consumer has printed the ten messages sent by the producer.

Pulsar Admin API

Pulsar is developed with REST-based APIs and JSON data exchange as a first-class protocol and not an afterthought. The API drives all admin functions. The pulsar-admin console relies on these APIs to deliver the intended outcomes. Additionally, there is a pulsar-admin Java client that builds custom workflows. Table 1-1 describes a few of the available major endpoints.

Table 1-1. *Pulsar Admin API*

Endpoint	Description
/admin/v2/clusters	Provides information about clusters
/admin/v2/brokers	Provides information about brokers
/admin/v2/tenants	Provides information about tenants
/admin/v2/namespaces	Provides information various namespaces

You work with each of these APIs in this book.

Summary

This chapter discussed enterprises building distributed platforms. Such platforms need event-driven architecture to handle various challenges of scalability, availability, and data consistency. You looked at Apache Pulsar, a powerful stream-processing platform. It has a layered architecture complemented by several out-of-the-box features, like multi-tenancy, zero rebalancing downtime, geo-replication, proxy and durability, and TLS-based authentication/authorization. You deployed Pulsar as single-node and multi-node clusters and looked at the API available with Pulsar. In the next chapter, you work with Pulsar client libraries to create various producers and consumers.

CHAPTER 2

Working with Messages

Messages have always been an integral part of programming and architecture design. This chapter outlines Apache Pulsar's message architecture and communication strategies. Let's begin by exploring the types of messages.

Types of Messages

Let's consider any two machines, or users, or even code fragments. A message can be defined as an exchange of information between a sender and one or more receivers.

Essentially, a message is an independent, discrete packet or bundle of data that the sender intends to send to one or more recipients.

The format of the data contained in the message does not matter. It can be anything, including a byte array, XML, JSON, or protobuf. Any type of data can be sent over the same channel, including the following.

- **Event message**: Notifies about an event; for example, a change in the state of the sender, such as the file preparation for download has completed or the upload of a document on a web page has completed.

- **Command message**: A regular message that contains a command to be run by the receiver; for example, a Simple Object Access Protocol (SOAP) request is a command message. This type of message expects the receiver to invoke a particular action.

- **Document message**: A simple message that contains data. It is up to the user to decide how to interpret and what to do with the data. It can be a text message to be processed by the recipients, such as an SMS, or a news broadcast containing the title, image(s), category, and a text description.

© Rahul Sharma and Mohammad Atyab 2022
R. Sharma and M. Atyab, *Cloud-Native Microservices with Apache Pulsar*,
https://doi.org/10.1007/978-1-4842-7839-0_2

Let's take the analogy of a courier parcel to describe a message. A parcel has the sender's address, delivery address, and the details of the good. When all the details are available, the parcel can be sent and received successfully. Similarly, a message can have metadata information or message headers and the actual data.

Message Channel

A channel is the media or communication link for transmitting messages between two endpoints that move messages (see Figure 2-1). Whenever two applications need to send data to each other, it is achieved through a messaging channel that connects them. A channel may have one-to-one, one-to-many, many-to-one, or many-to-many relationships among nodes.

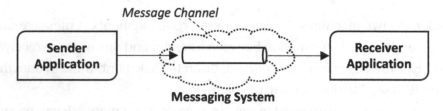

Figure 2-1. *Messaging system*

An application that needs to send data to another application does not toss the message directly to the other application but adds the message to a message channel. The receiver application has access to the same channel and reads the message from the channel.

The following are various examples of messaging channels.

- Queue channel

- Publisher-subscriber channel

- Priority channel

- Direct channel or point-to-point communication channel

Breaking up of Messages

If large messages need to be sent, they may need to be broken into multiple messages and sent in a sequence.

Asynchronous messaging is fundamentally a pragmatic reaction to distributed system problems. Sending a message does not require both systems to be up and ready at the same time. Furthermore, thinking about communication asynchronously forces developers to recognize that working with a remote application is slower, encouraging the design of components with high cohesion (lots of work locally) and low adhesion (selective work remotely).

Messaging Patterns

The message architecture has seen a lot of evolution over the last few years. Let's go through a few of them.

Point-2-Point

In this type of message, there is one-to-one direct channel-based communication. The two main entities are senders and consumers, and they exchange messages through a message queue. The senders push messages to a queue, and the consumers pick messages from the queue. The main feature of this type of communication is that the sender chooses the destination and is aware of the receiver. Only one consumer consumes a message. Although there can be multiple consumers, one message is intended for only one consumer. Therefore, the system has less decoupling.

A point-to-point messaging system can be more complex than it meets the eye. Here, multiple senders can send to multiple consumers. The connection for these messages may or may not be different, but the message queue is shared. As the message is put in a queue, the producer can go offline, and the consumer can still receive messages. The messages that consumers receive are in the order that they are sent in, but in some cases, the priority queue can be used, and thus the receiver can receive messages in a different order. The priority can be based on message expiry time, priority, and so on.

This is to be noted that there is no coupling between the consumers and the producer. Both the receiver and the consumer can be dynamically added or deleted at runtime.

Pub/Sub

Pub/Sub is a messaging pattern where messages are passed from a source, known as the *publisher*, to a destination, known as the *subscriber*. In this model, there are two main components: a publisher and one or more subscribers. The publisher has the responsibility of sending out messages on one more topic. The subscribers subscribe to the topic(s) and receive the messages sent out by the publisher. The salient point is that the publisher does not need to know who the subscribers are. It simply emits the events, knowing that the wider system needs them. Any application that wants the publisher's information may subscribe. It does not need to know the publisher or the other subscribers. Therefore, Pub/Sub is truly decoupled.

Take the example of a news service that reports on a variety of topics. A reader wants to be notified only about the topics they are interested in. In this scenario, you need a message mechanism that can send readers only what they have subscribed to, and Pub/Sub is an efficient solution.

In comparison to point-to-point messaging, the consumer does not have to listen in a queue. Instead, Pub/Sub is a push-based mechanism, and subscribers receive messages without requesting them.

Figure 2-2 shows how producers send data on a topic and how the consumers that subscribe to this topic receive the messages.

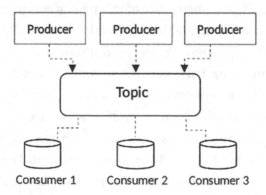

Figure 2-2. *Publisher-subscriber model*

The following are some of the advantages of Pub/Sub communication.

- **Simplification of communication**: All point-to-point connections are removed, and there is a single connection to the topic.

- **Loose coupling:** Compared to the client-server paradigm, where the clients and server both need to be up and running to communicate, the publisher is loosely coupled to every subscriber. Publishers and subscribers exist independently of each other, and the topic is the main focus.

- **Dynamic targeting:** As the service discovery is easier, any subscriber can easily subscribe to a topic and stop whenever they want, or they can change or update the subscription whenever they want. The publisher does not need to maintain a list of subscribers.

- **Code maintenance** becomes easier and simpler.

- **Scalability:** Pub/Sub systems provide opportunities to scale the systems by parallel processing, cache management, routing, and so forth.

To make sure the message reaches the desired subscribers, Pub/Sub uses message filtering.

Message Filtering

In the publish-subscribe model, subscribers can be configured to receive only a subset of the total messages published by the publishers. This process of selecting messages for reception and then processing is called *filtering*. Filtering can be applied in three ways: a topic-based system, a content-based system, or a hybrid system that leverages both.

- **Topic-based system:** Topics are named logical channels. Some subscribers subscribe to one or more topics, and some publishers publish messages on these topics. Every message is published for a topic. Filtering is achieved by subscribing to a subset of topics, and the subscribers receive only the messages for the topics they have subscribed to.

- **Content-based system:** The subscriber can define some constraints. Only those messages are delivered to a subscriber if the attributes or the complete message match the constraints defined by the subscriber. In this system, it is the responsibility of the subscriber to classify the messages.

- **Hybrid system**: A combination of the two systems can also be used by applications. The subscriber receives the messages to which they subscribe, and with that, they also specify the content attributes of the messages.

Pub/Sub subscriptions can be defined at the time of setup as either durable or non-durable. This defines the behavior of the system when the subscribers are terminated. Let us look at these subscriptions now.

Durable Subscriptions

To use persistent subscriptions, the subscriber needs to be durable. That means the subscriber should be given a name and should be registered by the messaging server. In this way, the server can remember the subscriber even if the system crashes or the subscriber itself crashes. In a scenario where a durable subscriber is disconnected, all the messages intended to be sent are stored. On reconnection, the subscriber receives all the messages it was supposed to receive.

Consider an application that sends emails to millions of users. Each email message is sent to the application and a "sender" microservice using Pub/Sub mode. Message flow can stop if the sender application or main application crashes and emails are not sent to users. In this example, a durable subscription can do the trick.

Non-Durable Subscriptions

A non-durable subscription is a connection in which the subscriber receives the messages only when it is alive. Messages delivered when the subscriber is not actively connected are lost. The broker queue may or may not save the messages. This can be useful if there are many topics with short-lived subscriptions that last minutes to hours, and then once data is read, the topic is no longer needed. If a user is active, a durable subscription for a chat room is created. If that user closes the browser, then the messages sent for this user fail, and there is no need to resend these messages.

Here, the messages are either delivered immediately or are not delivered at all. Therefore, there are only two states: connected or disconnected.

As an example, take a mobile application which on being active, subscribes to news topics. If it is alive, it can receive messages, but they should not be delivered on the application being closed or in sleep mode. The application can leverage non-durable subscriptions in this case.

Pulsar Client Libraries

Pulsar has client APIs with Java, Go, Python, and C++. The client API encapsulates and optimizes Pulsar's client-broker communication protocol. It also exposes a simple and intuitive API for use by the applications.

The current official Pulsar client libraries support transparent reconnection and connection failover to brokers, queuing of messages until acknowledged by the broker. These also consist of heuristics such as connection retries with backoff.

Client Setup Phase

When an application wants to create a producer/consumer, the Pulsar client library initiates a setup phase.

1. The client attempts to determine the topic's owner by sending an HTTP lookup request to the broker. The application could reach an active broker, which looks at ZooKeeper's cached metadata, and lets the user know about the topic or assigns it to the least-loaded broker.

2. Once the client library has the broker address, it creates a TCP connection (or authenticates an existing connection from the pool). Within this connection, binary commands are exchanged between the broker and the client from a custom protocol. The client sends a command to create a consumer or producer to the broker, which complies after the user validates the authorization policy.

This book uses Java Spring Boot.

To use a Pulsar client in Java, you need to add a dependency. At the time of writing this book, the latest stable version of Pulsar was 2.8.1.

```
<dependency>
    <groupId>org.apache.pulsar</groupId>
```

```
    <artifactId>pulsar-client</artifactId>
    <version>2.8.1</version>
</dependency>
```

Once this is added, the next step is to write the relevant classes that create and use the Pulsar client.

As mentioned in Chapter 1, you need to start the Pulsar server. For the sake of simplicity, run the server using the following command.

```
bin/pulsar standalone
```

Using a client with the provided server is the next step.

```
private static final String PULSAR_SERVICE_URL = "pulsar://localhost:6650";

public PulsarClient connectToClient() throws PulsarClientException {
    return PulsarClient.builder()
                .serviceUrl(PULSAR_SERVICE_URL)
                .build();
}
```

The client must be connected to both the publisher and the subscribers. Once a successful connection is made, you can move to the next step.

Creating a Producer

The task of publishing (generating messages) is a process handled by the *producer*. A publisher posts a message to the broker, and then the broker passes the message to the relevant consumers. When creating a producer, the broker verifies whether this client is authorized to publish on the topic. After confirmation, messages can be published to the broker.

To publish messages, you need to create a publisher, specify the topic and message, and publish the messages to the message broker. The consumers who have subscribed to the topic receive the messages. This example publishes new topics by category.

```
public boolean publishMessages(String category, NewsRequest newsRequest) {
    //use pulsar publish
    String MQ_TOPIC = "persistent://public/default/" + category;
```

```
try {
    PulsarClient client = connectToClient();
    Producer<byte[]> producer = client.newProducer()
            .topic(MQ_TOPIC)
            .create();
    producer.newMessage()
            .key("title")
            .value(newsRequest.getTitle().getBytes())
            .property("description", newsRequest.getDescription())
            .send();

    producer.close();
    client.close();
} catch (PulsarClientException e) {
    e.printStackTrace();
}
return true;
}
```

The first step is to connect the Pulsar client. After successfully doing so, a producer object is created with the topic name. A publisher is created, specifying the topic, and the messages it must send are created with keys and values. The send() method is called, which ultimately pushes the messages to the message broker.

The messages can be produced as sync or async.

- **Send sync**: The producer sends the message and waits for an acknowledgment. The message is treated as a failure if no acknowledgment is received.

```
producer.newMessage()
        .key("title")
        .value(newsRequest.getTitle().getBytes())
        .property("description", newsRequest.getDescription())
        .property("category", "sports")
        .sequenceId(123)
        .eventTime(System.currentTimeMillis())
        .send();
//removed for brevity
```

- **Send async**: The message is put in a blocking queue and
  CompletableFuture is returned. It is completed on receiving the
  acknowledgment or on error, and the end-user code can choose to
  wait on it. This allows for more inflight messages, which improves
  throughput.

```
producer.newMessage()
        .key("title")
        .value(newsRequest.getTitle().getBytes())
        .property("description", newsRequest.getDescription())
        .property("category", "sports")
        .sequenceId(123)
        .eventTime(System.currentTimeMillis())
        .sendAsync().thenRun(() -> {
    log.info("Message has been sent");
}).exceptionally(ex -> {
    log.warn("Message sending failed", ex);
});
//removed for brevity
```

Creating Consumers

As discussed, you need to create consumers who subscribe to a topic and consume the
published messages later.

```
public boolean subscribe(Category category) {
    String MQ_TOPIC = "persistent://public/default/" + category;

    try {
        PulsarClient client = connectToClient();
        ConsumerBuilder<byte[]> consumerBuilder = client.newConsumer()
                .topic(MQ_TOPIC)
                .subscriptionName(category.name())
                .subscriptionType(SubscriptionType.Shared)
                .messageListener(UserService::received);

        // Create three consumers (mq-consumer-0, mq-consumer-1, etc.)
```

```
        for (int i = 0; i < 3 ; i++) {
            String name = String.format("mq-consumer-%d", i);
            consumerBuilder
                    .consumerName(name)
                    .subscribe();
        }
    } catch (PulsarClientException e) {
        e.printStackTrace();
    }
    return true;
}

public static void received(Consumer<byte[]> consumer,
                    Message<byte[]> msg) {

    consumer.acknowledgeAsync(msg.getMessageId());
    // Do something with the received message
}
```

MQ_TOPIC is the topic to which the consumers subscribe.

The first step in creating consumer(s) is defining a consumer builder object. The builder is provided with the topic name, subscription name, type, listener method, and received method. Every time the publisher publishes a message on the subscribed topic(s), received is called with the consumer object and message object.

Here, three consumers consume messages in a loop in which the subscriber's name is changed. ConsumerBuilder is called with name, and subscribe is called.

The consumer can also receive messages using sync and async methods.

- **Receive sync**: A consumer call receives messages and blocks the call until a message is received.

```
Consumer consumer = client.newConsumer()
        .topic(topicNameStr)
        .subscriptionName(subscriptionNameStr)
        .subscribe();
consumer.receive();
```

- **Receive async**: A consumer receives messages in a future callback, like CompletableFuture in Java.

```
consumer.receiveAsync().thenAccept(msg -> {
    log.info("Received Msg:" + (String)msg);
});
```

Publish Messages

For publishing messages, you need to create a publisher, specify the topic and message, and publish the messages to the message broker. The consumers who have subscribed to the topic receive the messages. This example publishes new topics by category.

```
public boolean publishMessages(String category, NewsRequest newsRequest) {
    //use pulsar publish
    String MQ_TOPIC = "persistent://public/default/" + category;
    try {
        PulsarClient client = connectToClient();
        Producer<byte[]> producer = client.newProducer()
                .topic(MQ_TOPIC)
                .create();
        producer.newMessage()
                .key("title")
                .value(newsRequest.getTitle().getBytes())
                .property("description", newsRequest.getDescription())
                .send();

        producer.close();
        client.close();
    } catch (PulsarClientException e) {
        e.printStackTrace();
    }
    return true;
}
```

The first step is to connect the Pulsar client, and on successfully doing so, a producer object is created with the topic name. The publisher is created, specifying the topic. The messages it must send are created with keys and values. The send() method is called, which ultimately pushes the messages to the message broker.

The next topic discusses messages.

Messaging in Pulsar

The key components in Pulsar messaging are *producers* and *consumers*. The smallest unit of communication in Pulsar is a *message*. Let's look at a message in Pulsar. A message contains the following parts.

- **Value/data payload**: This is the actual data. The data is raw bytes by default, but there is an option to decide and register a schema to which the data needs to conform to. Schema Registry is discussed later in this book.

- **Key**: This is optional. The message can be tagged with keys. This can be useful for topic compaction and routing to partitions for ordering over any given key.

- **Properties**: The user can optionally define a key/value map of properties.

- **Producer name**: The message contains the name of the producer. If not specified, the default name would be shown.

- **Sequence ID**: Pulsar sends messages in order, and every message contains a sequence ID accordingly.

- **Publish time**: The epoch timestamp at which the message was published. The publisher automatically sets it.

- **Event time**: An optional timestamp that can be inserted and used by the application. If this is not set, the value is 0.

In a Java client, the message can be built using TypedMessageBuilder, as follows.

```
Producer<byte[]> producer = client.newProducer()
        .topic(MQ_TOPIC)
        .create();

producer.newMessage()
        .key("title")
        .value(newsRequest.getTitle().getBytes())
        .property("description", newsRequest.getDescription())
        .property("category", "sports")
        .sequenceId(123)
        .eventTime(System.currentTimeMillis())
        .send();
```

The default size of a message is 5 MB, but the maximum size of the message can be configured.

The following configures a broker.conf file size.

```
# The max size of a message (in bytes).
maxMessageSize=5242880
```

The following configures a bookkeeper.conf file size.

```
# The max size of the netty frame (in bytes). Any messages received larger
than this value are rejected. The default value is 5 MB.
nettyMaxFrameSizeBytes=5253120
```

Message Topic Format

In Pulsar, message topics are created as a URL using the following format.

{persistent|non-persistent}://tenant/namespace/topic

For example, persistent://public/default/sports

The following describes the parts of the URL.

- **persistent** or **non-persistent**: The first part denotes whether the messages are persistent or non-persistent.

- **Persistent**: When a subscriber reconnects (opens an existing subscription), messages received by the topic during the inactive period are delivered to the subscriber. This allows topic subscribers to take advantage of persistent messages.

- **Non-persistent**: Non-persistent topics are not written to the disk; instead, they are kept in memory. The messages are sent directly to the subscriber without persisting them in the message broker. All the messages are killed when the connection between the subscriber and the message broker is lost.

- **tenant**: Pulsar was created keeping multi-tenancy in mind. In a multi-tenant architecture, the multiple instances operate in a shared environment, allowing each tenant's data to be separated from one another. Tenants can be used in a clustered manner and can have their own authentication and authorization mechanism. Additionally, you can specify the storage quotas, isolation policy, and message TTL.

  In Pulsar, an instance can have multiple tenants. An instance is a group of Pulsar clusters (i.e., a set of brokers and BookKeeper, which may or may not reside in multiple geographical locations). As discussed earlier, a message topic can have a tenant. Multi-tenancy is useful in real-world applications. For example, for application 1, one tenant is used, and the statistics and billing for that application can be kept separate from application 2.

Using Pulsar admin APIs, tenants can be created, updated, and deleted. You read more about these APIs in Chapter 8.

By default, the value of the tenant is kept public.

- **namespace**: Within a tenant, there can be multiple namespaces. It is an administrative unit within a tenant. The topic needs to specify the namespace on which the topic is being published and subscribed.

By default, the value of the namespace is kept as default

- **topic**: The name of the exact topic for which the message is being published/subscribed.

Subscriptions

The management of consumers and messages is done using subscriptions. It tracks the messages that need to be delivered to one or more consumers. When connecting to Pulsar, the consumer needs to specify the subscription it is using. After the message is read and the consumer sends an acknowledgment, the read position in the topic is automatically updated.

There are several subscription types, including shared, key_shared, exclusive, and failover.

Shared

Multiple consumers configured on the same or different applications can subscribe to the same topic and consume from the same topic simultaneously (see Figure 2-3). The messages are sent in a round-robin manner to each connected consumer. If your application can be horizontally scaled, you can use the shared subscription to distribute the work to multiple instances of the application. The subscription does not guarantee any messaging order, and cumulative acknowledgment cannot be used in this type of subscription.

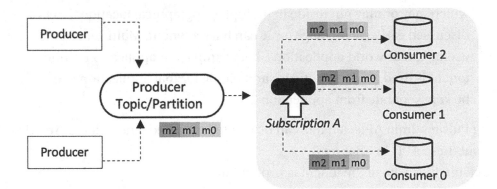

Figure 2-3. *Shared subscription*

The following code snippet shows three consumers (news readers for this example) listening on the same topic with a shared subscription. When a message on a topic is sent, it is delivered to relevant consumers according to subscriptions and filtering. Let's see an example of consumer creation (only a relevant section of the code is kept for the sake of brevity).

```
//creation of consumer builder
ConsumerBuilder<byte[]> consumerBuilder = client.newConsumer()
                .topic(MQ_TOPIC)
                .subscriptionName(category.name())
                .subscriptionType(SubscriptionType.Shared)
                .messageListener(UserService::received);

        // Create three consumers
        for (int i = 0; i < 3 ; i++) {
            String name = String.format("mq-consumer-%d", i);
            consumerBuilder
                    .consumerName(name)
                    .subscribe();
        }
    } catch (PulsarClientException e) {
        e.printStackTrace();
    }
    return true;
}

public static void received(Consumer<byte[]> consumer,
Message<byte[]> msg) {
    // Do something with the received message
}
```

Pulsar can be used as a scalable messaging queue using a shared subscription. The key idea is to use the built-in load balancing of Pulsar and set the queue size very low (it can be set at 0 as well).

Consider an ecommerce website that produces new order updates from the front end and then sends information to consumers through a customer relationship management (CRM) software solution, a marketing solution, an ad platform, and so on. Since you want the data to be sent to all these services, you can configure multiple consumer applications to get this information using a shared subscription.

Key_Shared

Like a shared subscription except all messages with the same key are delivered to the same consumer (see Figure 2-4), which allows the following.

- Building aggregated states

- Better key-based local caches

- Easy scalability for sharded services

```
private final Consumer<String> consumer;
public static HashedConsumer(final List<Range> ranges,
                                       final int partitionIndex) throws
PulsarClientException {
    consumer = client.newConsumer(Schema.STRING)
            .subscriptionMode(SubscriptionMode.Durable)
            .topic(topicNameStr)
            .consumerName("Consumer: " + partitionIndex)
            .subscriptionName("hashed-key-subscription")
            .subscriptionType(SubscriptionType.Key_Shared)

.keySharedPolicy(KeySharedPolicy.stickyHashRange().ranges(ranges.toArray
(new Range[ranges.size()])))
            .subscribe();

}
```

The key shared policy can be either sticky or auto. In sticky hashing, the hash range for the consumer is user-defined. Each consumer is bound to the hash range, and the only messages it can consume any message are the hash range specified. A use case of the sticky hash range is sharded cache services. In auto hashing, Pulsar distributes hashes across consumers and handles rebalancing.

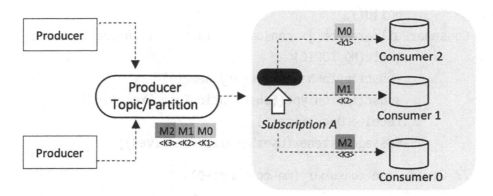

Figure 2-4. *Key_Shared subscription*

Exclusive

Only one consumer can take a subscription in this type of subscription; another is not allowed. They get an error when trying to do so (see Figure 2-5).

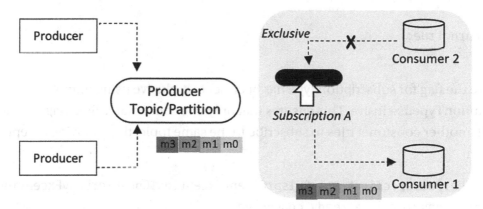

Figure 2-5. *Exclusive subscription*

Let's use the shared subscription example. A subscription can be made exclusive by making the following changes.

```
public boolean subscribe(Category category) {
    String MQ_TOPIC = "persistent://public/default/" + category;
    PulsarClient client = null;
    try {
        client = PulsarClient.builder()
                .serviceUrl(PULSAR_SERVICE_URL)
```

```
                .build();
       ConsumerBuilder<byte[]> consumerBuilder = client.newConsumer()
               .topic(MQ_TOPIC)
               .subscriptionName(category.name())
               .subscriptionType(SubscriptionType.Exclusive)
               .receiverQueueSize(5)
               .messageListener(UserService::received);

       // Create one consumer (mq-consumer-0)

           String name = "mq-consumer-0";
           consumerBuilder
                   .consumerName(name)
                   .subscribe();
    } catch (PulsarClientException e) {
        e.printStackTrace();
    }
    return true;
}
```

Here the flag for subscription type has been set to exclusive using Enum SubscriptionType.Exclusive. This ensures that only one consumer is listening for one topic. If another consumer tries to subscribe to the same topic, the following exception is thrown:

```
org.apache.pulsar.client.api.PulsarClientException$ConsumerBusyException:
Exclusive consumer is already connected
```

For example, a user must receive messages in a mailbox, and to do so, an exclusive subscription to their mail can do the trick.

Failover

Multiple consumers are attached to the same topic, but there are never two active consumers at once (see Figure 2-6). These consumers are sorted lexically with names. The first consumer is the master consumer and gets all the messages. When the master consumer is disconnected, the next consumers get the messages.

Note the following code:

```
ConsumerBuilder<byte[]> consumerBuilder = client.newConsumer()
        .topic(MQ_TOPIC)
        .subscriptionName(category.name())
        .subscriptionType(SubscriptionType.Failover)
        .messageListener(UserService::received);

// Create three consumers (mq-consumer-0, mq-consumer-1, etc.)
for (int i = 0; i < 3 ; i++) {
    String name = String.format("mq-consumer-%d", i);
    consumerBuilder
            .consumerName(name)
            .subscribe();
}
```

In this case, there are three consumers, but they have a failover subscription. Therefore, only mq-consumer-0 receives the messages, and when it disconnects, the next consumer, mq-consumer-1 receives the messages, and so on.

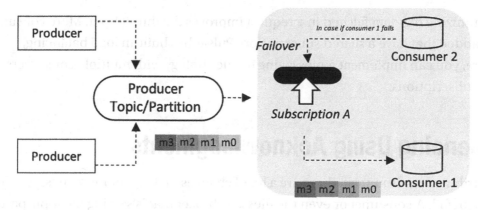

Figure 2-6. *Failover subscription*

For example, take an ecommerce website that produces a new order update from the front end and sends information to a consumer that updates the order data into the CRM. Since you want the update in the CRM, you can configure so that multiple consumers to get information using a failover subscription.

Receiver Queues

When a message is available in a queue, the consumer receives that and tries to process it. But there are cases when the number of messages being received is greater than the messages the consumer can process. When the consumer loses connection and when it comes back, it should receive the messages it lost. There should be a backlog of messages that the consumer can look up and read to achieve this. In such scenarios, the messages are stored in queues in the same order same they are received. By default, the number of messages that a consumer can hold in a queue is 1000. This also means that the number of messages the consumer can fetch at a time is 1000.

A queue size for a can also be tweaked by changing the consumer's configuration. The following is a consumer with a small receiver queue.

```
ConsumerBuilder<byte[]> consumerBuilder = client.newConsumer()
        .topic(MQ_TOPIC)
        .subscriptionName(category.name())
        .subscriptionType(SubscriptionType.Shared)
        .receiverQueueSize(5)
        .messageListener(UserService::received);
```

Minimizing the data fetched in a request improves the throughput. More consumers can be added that have a shared subscription. Pulsar has built-in load balancing, therefore, you can implement a messaging queue strategy with multiple consumers with shared subscriptions.

Sequencing Using Acknowledgments

In a distributed environment, there are a lot of chances that one or more messages from a topic can fail. A consumer or even the message broker that is serving the topic partition may fail.

In such a scenario, you can resume the consumption of messages from the point where the consumption has failed. Apache Pulsar uses cursors for tracking the message acknowledgment of each subscription. Whenever a consumer confirms a message on the topic partition, the cursor is updated and ensures that the consumer does not receive the same message again. Messages can be confirmed in two ways: through individual confirmation acknowledgment or cumulative confirmation message. For sending a cumulative confirmation, the consumer needs to confirm only the last message it received. Afterward, all messages in the topic partition, including the provided message ID, are marked, and the consumer does not receive those messages again.

In the previous example, you can send cumulative acknowledgment in the following manner.

```
public static void received(Consumer<byte[]> consumer,
                    Message<byte[]> msg) {

    consumer.acknowledgeCumulative((msg.getMessageId());

    // Do something with the received message
}
//Remaining code has been removed for brevity
```

Similarly, messages can be acknowledged individually. This can be considered as selective acknowledgment. The consumer has the power to select the message that they want to acknowledge. These messages are not delivered again. Figure 2-7 illustrates how cumulative acks are sent. Grayed-out messages in the figure are confirmed and are not delivered again. On receiving M3, the system confirms that M0, M1, M2, and M3 have been delivered. Similarly, on receiving M8, it is confirmed that the consumer has received messages M4 to M8.

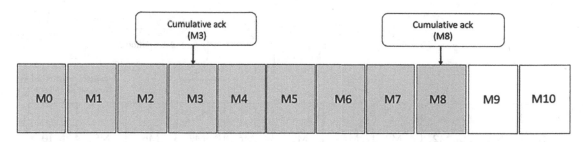

Figure 2-7. *Cumulative acknowledgments and individual acknowledgments*

Consumers in shared subscriptions cannot use cumulative acknowledgments as shared mode involves multiple consumers having access to the same subscription. The acknowledgment processing for every message is cumbersome for many applications, and it would force excess load on the system. Thus, cumulative acknowledgment helps enable the applications to handle consumer failures in a better manner.

Cumulative acknowledgment messages are allowed to be sent in case of exclusive and failover subscriptions.

The ability to individually confirm messages provides a better experience for handling consumer failures. For some applications, processing those confirmed messages may be very time-consuming, and it is very important to prevent retransmission of confirmed messages.

```
public static void received(Consumer<byte[]> consumer,
                    Message<byte[]> msg) {

    consumer.acknowledgeAsync(msg.getMessageId());


    // Do something with the received message
}
//Remaining code has been removed for brevity
```

Message Retention

In Pulsar, there is a significant difference from the traditional system. The messages are not deleted immediately after acknowledgment is received (see Figure 2-8). They are deleted only when all the acks of all the subscribers have been received. Till that time, they are marked as confirmed only. Pulsar also gives the capability to keep the messages retained for a longer duration as well.

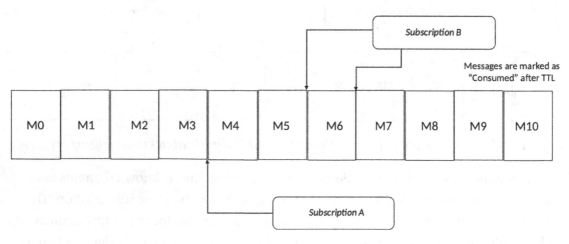

Figure 2-8. *Message retention and TTL*

Time-to-Live (TTL)

Pulsar provides time-to-live (TTL) to every message. If the message is not consumed within a set TTL, it is marked as consumed. As opposed to message retention, which is applied at the topic level, the TTL is applied at the message level.

Retention Policy

The "message is deleted once it is acknowledged" rule doesn't satisfy Pulsar's data streaming use case. Messages must be kept for Pulsar's reader interface and logging purposes.

This is where Pulsar's retention policy helps. Pulsar is asked to retain acknowledged messages and messages on a topic with no subscription and then these messages are not deleted. The configuration parameters that help to do so are in the broker.conf file: defaultRetentionTimeInMinutes and defaultRetentionTimeInSize.

Retention policy mainly defines

- The limit to keeping acknowledged events

- Mark messages over the limit as deleted

The retention policies are applied at the namespace level, therefore different namespaces can have different policies.

Backlog Quota

Any unacknowledged messages for a particular subscription in a backlog are retained. This means the following.

- All unacknowledged messages are retained in a subscription backlog.

- When messages in a backlog are acknowledged, they are removed from the backlog and marked for deletion.

The maximum backlog permitted size can be set for a topic. This is defined by the backlogQuotaDefaultLimitGB parameter in a broker.conf file. It sets a limit on the maximum backlog size that is permitted for the topic. As one topic can have multiple backlogs, Pulsar applies the limit to the largest subscription backlog for the topic (i.e., from the slowest consumer).

Pulsar can remove old messages when the topic backlog size limit is reached or message transmission may be interrupted. Pulsar has the following policies for the prevention of backlog overflow.

- **producer_request_hold**: The producer's send request is held until the backlog has space for more messages. The producer send() method is blocked until one of the following conditions are met.

  - Producer send() method times out

  - New consumer acknowledgments are received that take messages off the backlog, thereby freeing space in the backlog

- **producer_exception**: ProducerBlockedQuotaExceededException is received in Java code while publishing a message.

- **consumer_backlog_eviction**: There is only one logical copy of a message. Both message acknowledgment and TTL move a cursor to track messages consumption on a backlog.

In the first two options, message transmission is interrupted, and any further backlog growth is prevented. Consumers can still receive and acknowledge existing messages.

In the third option, the existing messages are deleted from the backlog. There is a 0.9 reduction factor consumer_backlog_eviction has a for message eviction. Therefore, 10% of the oldest messages in the backlog are deleted for the slowest consumer. Neither the producers nor the consumers receive any exceptions or errors, and message transmission continues as usual. The same design as Pulsar moves the subscription cursor to skip messages in the backlog is followed in this policy. The skipped messages are still available for the reader interface if the retention policy is correctly configured.

The default broker option is producer_request_hold, and it is the least intrusive preference as it relies mainly on consumers to drain the backlog.

Batching and Chunking

Accumulation and sending of messages at one go (i.e., in single request) is called *batching*. Chunking is the opposite of batching. One message is split into multiple messages when a message size exceeds the maximum message size of the Broker configuration. Let's look at these two actions in more detail now.

Batching

The batch size is defined by the maximum number of messages and the maximum publish latency. Considering backlog, the size in the backlog is the size of the batches.

The following are salient features of batching in Pulsar.

- **Tracking**: The batches are considered single units; therefore, their storage and tracking are done per batch, not individual messages. Consumer unbundles a batch into individual messages.

- **Acknowledgment**: A batch is considered acknowledged when all the messages in the batch are acknowledged by the consumer(s).

However, the messages that are sent can also be scheduled using the `deliverAt` and `deliverAfter` parameters. If messages are sent in a batch, the parameters take precedence, and the messages are scheduled accordingly. The following is a code example to enable batching.

```
ProducerBuilder<byte[]> builder = client.newProducer()
    .enableBatching(true)
    .messageRoutingMode(MessageRoutingMode.SinglePartition)
    .batchingMaxPublishDelay(10, TimeUnit.MILLISECONDS)
    .batchingMaxMessages(10);
```

You can see that the producer can be set to enable batching using the `enableBatching` flag. The publish delay and max batch size can be set using `batchingMaxPublishDelay` and `batchingMaxMessages`, respectively.

A drawback of using batching is in an unexpected failure, or a negative acknowledgment, or acknowledgment timeouts. In this case, Pulsar resends all the messages in the batch, even if the consumer acknowledges some of them.

Batch Index Acknowledgment

Pulsar 2.6.0 introduced batch index acknowledgment to avoid redelivery of the acknowledged messages to the consumer. In batch index acknowledgment, the following happens.

1. During receiving, the consumer filters out the batch index that has been acknowledged, and then it sends the batch index acknowledgment request to the message broker.

2. The broker maintains a batch index acknowledgment status. The tracking of the acknowledgment status of each batch index to avoid dispatching acknowledged messages to the consumer is also done.

3. The batch message is deleted when all the batch message's indexes are acknowledged.

At the broker side, the setting that needs to be enabled is acknowledgmentAtBatchIndexLevelEnabled = true. This needs to be updated manually because the state is disabled by default.

The disadvantage of batch index acknowledgment enabling is that it results in more memory overhead.

Batch Receiving in Consumers

Since the 2.4.1 version of Pulsar, a consumer can also be set to receive messages in batches. You can set the consumer to get messages in bulk using the BatchReceivePolicy class. This is described using the following code example.

```
Consumer<GenericRecord> consumer = pulsarClient
        .newConsumer(Schema.AUTO_CONSUME())
        .batchReceivePolicy(BatchReceivePolicy.builder()
            .maxNumMessages(2000)
            .maxNumBytes(1024 * 1024)
            .timeout(10, TimeUnit.SECONDS).build())
```

Next, to get the messages in bulk, use batchReceive.

```
Messages<GenericRecord> batchMessages = consumer.batchReceive();
```

When all messages are processed, acknowledge all of them, as follows.

```
consumer.acknowledge(batchMessages);
```

Chunking

Once turned on, all the messages that are going outsize, the message size is broken, the producer is set to automatically use the chunking functionality, and the messages are split to make multiple small messages and sequentially sent to the broker in order. The following producer and consumer configurations need to completed before using chunking.

- Consumers can be set to use only non-shared subscriptions: exclusive or failover.

- The topics must be persistent.

- Batch mode needs to be disabled.

- Even after the broker has received the acknowledgment, the client can continue to send a message to the broker. maxPendingMessages configuration in the broker can be used to avoid overly high memory usage.

- Clean up of chunk messages can be done by configuring message TTL/retention. Some scenes, such as producer or broker restart, cause the broker to receive an incomplete chunk message. This part of the message consumer cannot be an acknowledgment. You need to be cleaned up according to TTL or retention.

- receiverQueueSize and maxPendingChunkedMessage can be configured at the consumer end.

There is no change required at the broker end to support chunking for non-shared subscription. It only uses chunkedMessageRate for recording chunked message rates on the topic.

All chunks have the same SequenceID and UUID. If a message size exceeds the maximum, then it is divided by default.

The following code is an example.

```
Producer<byte[]> producer = producerBuilder.enableChunking(true).
enableBatching(false)
          .create();
```

As you can see, chunking can be enabled using enableChunkingEnabled(true) in the producer builder. If the message size is greater than the allowed maximum publish-payload size, which can be set in the configuration of Pulsar, the producer splits the original message sent by the producer into multiple messages (i.e., chunks). They are published with chunked metadata to the broker separately and in order.

The chunked messages are treated the same way they are stored in the normal non-chunked messages at the broker end. It is the job of the consumer to receive and buffer the chunks into a real message. If publishing all the chunks is failed at the producer end, the consumer can expire incomplete chunks if the consumer fails to receive all chunks in expire time. The expire time is customizable, and it is set to one hour as the default.

At the consumer end, the consumer is responsible for receiving and re-creating the message after buffering them. After re-creating the message, the consumer puts it into a receiver queue, and the application client consumes messages from this receiver queue.

After receiving all the chunks, the consumer sends one acknowledgment for the message, but internally it sends acknowledgment for all the message's chunks. The maxPendingChunkedMessage configuration stating the number of pending chunks can be set. Once the pending messages reach this value, there are two things that the consumer can do.

- The non-received chunks are dropped by silently acknowledging them

- The non-received chunks are asked to be redelivered by marking them unacknowledged

Handle Chunked Messages with One Producer and One Ordered Consumer

Figure 2-9 illustrates that one producer sends messages, and one consumer consumes those messages. At the time of publishing, the M1 and M2 messages are chunked into multiple messages. The broker stores all the three chunked messages in the managed ledger and dispatches them to the consumers in the same receiving order. It remains the task of the consumer to stitch the messages back and make them usable.

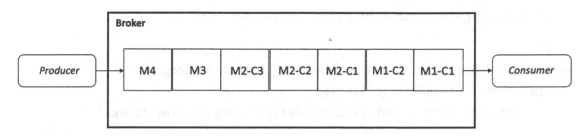

Figure 2-9. *Chunking with one producer and one consumer*

You can see that one producer is sending messages, and one consumer is consuming those messages. At the time of publishing, the M1 and M2 messages are chunked into multiple messages. The broker stores all the three chunked messages in the managed ledger and dispatches them to the consumers in the same receiving order. It remains the task of the consumer to stitch the messages back and make them usable.

Handle Chunked Messages with Multiple Producers and One Ordered Consumer

When multiple producers send multiple chunked messages, the broker first keeps these chunked messages into a managed ledger and sends them to the consumer. The ordering of the messages is kept intact, but they don't need to be kept consecutively. Figure 2-10 shows that the messages from producers 1 and 2 are not consecutive but are in the same order as they were produced. Now the consumer needs to receive, keep track of, and combine them into M1 and M2.

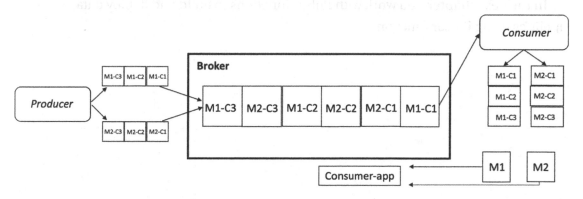

Figure 2-10. *Chunking with multiple producers and one consumer*

The following shows testing batching and chunking together.

```
@Test
public void testInvalidUseCaseForChunking() throws Exception {
    this.conf.setMaxMessageSize(5);
    String topicName = "persistent://default/namespace/my-topic1";

    ProducerBuilder<byte[]> producerBuilder = pulsarClient.newProducer().
    topic(topicName);

        Producer<byte[]> producer = producerBuilder.enableChunking(true).
        enableBatching(true).create();
        fail("it should fail because chunking can't be used with batching
        enabled");
}
```

Summary

This chapter covered the basics of messages in Pulsar and how to handle them in communication strategies like Pub/Sub. The basics of writing code for a Pulsar client in Java were also discussed. You worked on unified APIs for Pulsar, and operations like sequencing, acknowledgment, batching, and chunking were explained. Retention policies and TTL to easily build and maintain a robust application by tweaking parameters were also covered.

In the next chapter, you work with Pulsar functions to build and deploy data pipelines using Pulsar functions.

CHAPTER 3

Working with Pulsar Functions

The functional paradigm has matured into an architectural style that can be applied across various components, like infrastructure using serverless or server-side applications in various programming languages, such as Python, Node.js, Java, front-end UI, and reactive applications. This diversity can be attributed to the following benefits provided by a functional design.

- Improves modularity and cohesion

- Complex problem-solving

- Reduced redundancy

- Improved testability and maintainability

Apache Pulsar provides support for building functional data processors. In this chapter, you work with functional data processors that build multi-stage transformation pipelines. By the end of the chapter, you will be confident in creating and testing Pulsar Functions.

Functional Design

One of the ways to solve business workflow problems is to break down the entire cycle into smaller, simpler components. These individual autonomous components, also known as functions, have predictable behaviors and are easier to build because they are confined to limited responsibilities. Solutions developed using functional architecture offer the following business advantages.

© Rahul Sharma and Mohammad Atyab 2022
R. Sharma and M. Atyab, *Cloud-Native Microservices with Apache Pulsar*,
https://doi.org/10.1007/978-1-4842-7839-0_3

A breakdown provides insight into the different stages of the entire workflow. Every stage has its own input and output that determines its behavior for various supported scenarios. Thus, it provides the necessary information for analysis and demonstrates how different business conditions impact the end-to-end solution.

The compositional approach of a functional paradigm provides the flexibility to replace components, interchange components, and add missing components. Since each component is different, it can be developed using the most relevant frameworks. This yields agility to business solutions with a reduced time-to-market. This is beneficial for businesses that want to remain current with new technology as it evolves, allowing investments to be targeted and value-driven instead of transformational each time it looks to upgrade technology platforms. A functional architecture saves you from doing double the work.

Like all other methodologies, the functional methodology is also based on principles. Three principles establish practices that develop a solution architecture with considerations for extension and maintenance as the solution evolves. Adopting these practices can also contribute to avoiding pitfalls and reduced complexity.

The first principle is that a function is a stand-alone, autonomous component that provides behavior for a particular task in the business workflow (see Figure 3-1). Each task in a workflow represents a unit of data processing: filtering, transforming, and enriching data. These functions take input and provide output as configured by their deployment.

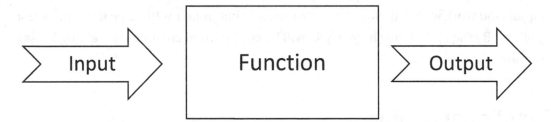

Figure 3-1. *Basic function*

In the second principle, composition is the primary way to build systems. Two functions can be composed by connecting the output of one to the input of another. Their result is represented as another function that can be used as a starting point for another composition.

From an architectural perspective, the most obvious consequence of composing bigger functions from smaller ones is that functional systems tend to look like pipelines with input and output rather than a message-oriented request/response model. Each task function generally has the same structure: data is read, business decisions are made, data is transformed as needed, and, finally, any new data or events are output at the other end (see Figure 3-2). Each of these steps can, in turn, be treated as a smaller function.

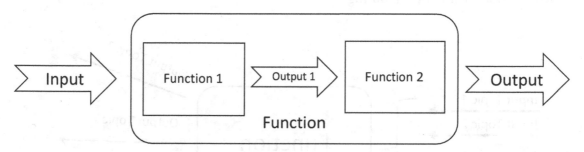

Figure 3-2. *Function composition*

This compositional approach means you only combine the specific components you need for a particular business workflow. There is no need for traditional layered architecture. As you add new features to a system, the functionality required for each new workflow is defined independently rather than grouped into a database or services layer.

In the third principle, functional programmers use pure functions as much as possible, given that the input always results in the same output. A pure function is deterministic and has no side effects. They are very easy to test and easy to understand without drilling into their implementation. When a function is "pure"—meaning it has no side effects—it can be written, tested, reasoned, and debugged in isolation, without the need to understand external context or the history of events surrounding its execution.

Pulsar Functions

Pulsar Functions can be classified as processing blocks that consume messages from one or more Pulsar topics, apply a user-defined logic to each incoming message, and publish the results to one or more topics (see Figure 3-3). All these features are provided out-of-the-box without the need for an external framework/system. The simplicity of Pulsar Functions makes them appropriate to handle many day-to-day uses, like ETL jobs, real-time aggregation, and event routing.

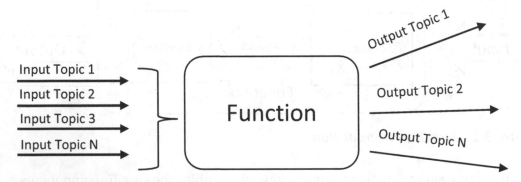

Figure 3-3. *Pulsar Functions*

Pulsar Functions are inspired by serverless solutions like AWS Lambda and Azure Functions. The serverless design allows developers to build and run applications without having to manage their infrastructure. Developers simply package their code in an appropriate format for deployment.

Pulsar Functions provide the necessary abstraction to develop application logic independent of any input and output Pulsar topics. The input and output topics are provided with the Pulsar Functions deployment configuration. Pulsar takes care of the underlying details required to run and scale your code with high availability. Pulsar Functions provides a ready-made computing infrastructure in your existing Pulsar cluster.

Pulsar Functions are lightweight compute processes that

- Execute each time a message is published on a specified input topic

- Apply user-supplied processing logic to each message

- Publish the results of the computation to one or more topics

> **Note**   Pulsar Functions offer simplicity for basic use cases, but you may require external frameworks like Apache Heron, Apache Storm, or Apache Flink for complex processing with enterprise integration.

Developing Function

Chapter 2 explained that Pulsar's official clients are the Java, Python, and Go programming languages. Pulsar Functions are supported only in these respective programming languages. You can create and deploy Pulsar Functions in either of these languages without a separate stream processing engine like Apache Flink.

Java, Python, and Go programming languages have native support for the functional paradigm. Pulsar Function can be created using language-native functional interfaces, thus doing away with any Pulsar-specific libraries or special dependencies.

> **Note**   Generate a Maven quick-start project (see Chapter 2) to develop the functions discussed in this chapter.

Let's build your first Pulsar function for substitution cipher encryption. A substitution cipher is one of the basic techniques to encrypt data. In this technique, each letter in a given text is replaced with a letter with a fixed number of positions down the alphabet. For example, with a shift of 1, A would be replaced by B, B would become C, and so on.

```
public class EcryptFunction implements Function<String, String> {

    private final int displacement = 4;

    @Override
    public String apply(String input) {
        String result = input.chars()
                .map(x -> {
                    int indexChar = (x > 96) ? 97 : 65;
                    int position = (x - indexChar) + displacement;
```

```
            return indexChar + (position % 26);
        })
        .mapToObj(i -> Character.toString((char)i))
        .collect(Collectors.joining());
    return result;
  }
}
```

The preceding function defines the substitution cipher function that does the following.

- It takes an input string and returns an encrypted string, which shifts each alphabet by four positions.

- It converts the string into a sequence of characters, with each character represented by its ASCII value.

- Uppercase alphabets are represented using ASCII code 65 to 90, and Lowercase alphabets are represented from 97 to 122. Each character is encrypted as per its ASCII representation.

- Finally, it converts all integer ASCII codes is to respective characters and concatenates them in a string.

Since the function is part of a Maven project, you can package it using the Maven build command.

```
$./mvnw clean install
```

The resultant JAR can then be deployed in Pulsar with appropriate input and output topics. The easiest way to run a Pulsar function is to instantiate a runtime and the function locally by using the local run mode.

In local run mode, the function runs as a stand-alone runtime on your workstation. Pulsar Functions command-line tool provides all required options to support this. You discuss function deployment in detail later in this chapter. For now, deploy the JAR file using the following command.

```
$ bin/pulsar-admin functions localrun   \
--jar  pulsar-functions/target/pulsar-functions-1.0-SNAPSHOT.jar   \
--classname EcryptFunction \
```

```
--name substitution-cypher   \
--inputs plaintext    \
--output ciphertext
```

This command uses the following options to configure the function.

- The --jar option specifies the path to the JAR file.

- The --classname option specifies the fully qualified class name of the function.

- The --name option configures a name for the deployed function.

- The --input option specifies topics for function input. The function read messages arriving on the topics specified.

- The --output option specifies topics for function output. The function sends messages on the topics specified.

You can pass a message by creating a console-based producer with input topic.

```
$ bin/pulsar-client produce plaintext --messages "AttackAtOnce"
```

You need to create a consumer on ciphertext topic can see the encrypted message on the ciphertext topic.

```
$ bin/pulsar-client consume ciphertext -s "message-reader" -n 0
key:[null], properties:[__pfn_input_msg_id__=CNMLEAEgADAB, __pfn_input_
topic__=persistent://public/default/plaintext], content:lipps>typyouv?>mxw>
vemrc>hec>xshec
22:41:18.318 [pulsar-timer-5-1] INFO  org.apache.pulsar.client.impl.
ConsumerStatsRecorderImpl - [ciphertext] [first-1-subscription] [3776c]
Prefetched messages: 0 --- Consume throughput received: 0.02 msgs/s ---
0.00 Mbit/s --- Ack sent rate: 0.02 ack/s --- Failed messages: 0 --- batch
messages: 0 ---Failed acks: 0
----- got message -----
key:[null], properties:[__pfn_input_msg_id__=CNMLEAIgADAB, __pfn_input_
topic__=persistent://public/default/plaintext], content:ExxegoExSrgi
```

Type Support

The following are basic, built-in Pulsar Functions in Java that are supported by default.

- String

- Double

- Integer

- Float

- Long

- Short

- Byte

Complex data types are supported using either protocol buffers, Avro or JSON Schema. By default, Pulsar works with JSON format. Let's explore the Schema support by developing a movie data ingestion process. The data is presented in delimited formatted and then transformed into a Movie object, which becomes the domain for further processing.

```java
public class Movie {
    private String title;
    private String genre;
    private String [] actors;
    private int ratings;

  // Removed for Brevity
}
```

The Movie domain object has properties related to name, genre, actors, and ratings. You have a simple function to convert the delimited data into a Movie object and send it as output.

```java
public class MovieIngestionFunction implements Function<String, Movie> {

    @Override
    public Movie apply(String delimited data) {
        String[] fields = delimetedData.split(":");
```

```
    String[] actors = Arrays.copyOfRange(fields, 3, fields.length);
    return new Movie(fields[0], fields[1], fields[2],  actors);
  }
}
```

The preceding code splits the input message using the colon character (:) as a delimiter. Then the data is converted in a Movie instance. Let's build the project and deploy the function using the command shown next.

```
$ bin/pulsar-admin functions localrun    \
--jar  pulsar-functions/target/pulsar-functions-1.0-SNAPSHOT.jar    \
--classname MovieIngestionFunction \
 --inputs movie-csv-data    \
 --output movie-data    \
 --name movie-reader
```

You can pass a delimited data on the movie-CSV-data topic using a console producer, as follows.

```
$ bin/pulsar-client produce movie-CSV-data --messages "Shrek:comedy:8:Mike
Myers:Eddie Murphy:Cameron Diaz"
```

The data is printed in JSON format on the console consumer as shown next.

```
$ bin/pulsar-client consume movie-details -s "movie-1-subscription" -n 0
22:43:01.402 [main] WARN  io.netty.resolver.dns.
DnsServerAddressStreamProviders - Can not find io.netty.resolver.dns.macos.
MacOSDnsServerAddressStreamProvider in the classpath, fallback to system
defaults. This may result in incorrect DNS resolutions on MacOS.

----- got message -----
key:[null], properties:[__pfn_input_msg_id__=CPQLEAEgADAB, __pfn_input_
topic__=persistent://public/default/movie-data], content:  {"name":"shrek",
"genre":"comedy", "actors":["Mike Myers","Eddie Murphy","Cameron Diaz"],
"ratings": 8}
```

Custom Serialization

Object serialization is the process of controlling the serialization and deserialization of a type. It can offer benefits for efficient data exchange while ensuring compatibility across different versions of a type without breaking the core functionality of the type.

Earlier, you worked with Pulsar-provided formats, but Pulsar Schema support is quite extensible which can be customized to support any required format. The Pulsar Functions SDK offers Schema support by using the SerDe interface for controlling serialization.

```
public interface SerDe<T> {
    T deserialize(byte[] var1);

    byte[] serialize(T var1);
}
```

There is only one requirement since Pulsar performs binary data exchange, so all types must be serialized and deserialized from a bytes array. Thus the interface methods are responsible for coveting the objects in byte[] since you convert it to the required type. Java Generics support makes sure that an instance is responsible for handling a particular type of conversion.

Going back to the movie domain example from the previous section, let's replace the JSON format with a custom format using Kryo. First, add the Function SDK using the following dependencies to the pom.xml.

```
<dependency>
    <groupId>org.apache.pulsar</groupId>
    <artifactId>pulsar-functions-api</artifactId>
    <version>${pulsar.version}</version>
</dependency>
```

Kryo is a Java serialization framework with a focus on speed, efficiency, and a user-friendly API. This book only covers basic uses and does not cover the framework in detail. Please refer to the framework's documentation to know more about it. Add a Kryo dependency to make sure you can work with the Kryo API for serialization.

```
<dependency>
    <groupId>com.esotericsoftware</groupId>
```

```
    <artifactId>kryo</artifactId>
    <version>5.1.1</version>
</dependency>
```

The Kryo API provides a simple API to convert an object into a byte array and vice versa.

```
@Override
public byte[] serialize(Movie movie) {
    ByteArrayOutputStream outStream = new ByteArrayOutputStream();
    Output kout = new Output(outStream);
    kryo.writeObject(kout, movie);
    kout.close();
    return outStream.toByteArray();
}
```

The preceding code does the following.

- Implements the serialize method, which takes an instance of a Movie object as a parameter.

- Uses the Kryo wroteObject API to convert an object into bytes.

- Writes the bytes to a Java BytesOutputsStream and returns the bytes from the stream.

```
@Override
public Movie deserialize(byte[] bytes) {
    Input kin = new Input(new ByteArrayInputStream(bytes));
    Movie movie = kryo.readObject(kin, Movie.class);
    return movie;
}
```

The preceding code does the following.

- Implements the deserialize method, which takes an instance of byte array as a parameter

- Creates an input stream to read the bytes

- Uses the Kryo readObject API to convert bytes into an object of the Movie class

As shown in the code, you are working with a pre-initialized instance of Kryo. Moreover, Kryo supports all Java basic types. Before invocation, complex types like domain classes, arrays, and collections must be registered with a Kryo instance.

```
private final Kryo kryo;
public MovieSrDe(){
    kryo = new Kryo();
    kryo.register(Movie.class);
    kryo.register(java.lang.String[].class);
}
```

This code configures Kryo in the default constructor of the implementation. It does the following.

- Creates an instance of Kryo

- Registers Movie.class with the instance

- Registers String[].class with the instance (the array is used for Movie properties)

You deployed a JAR of the project in previous examples because all examples relied on native-language libraries. But the code needs Kryo and Functions SDK dependencies to be available to work as expected. Instead of deploying a JAR project, Pulsar recommends deploying a JAR inclusive of dependencies. Thus, you add the following maven-assembly-plugin configuration to build it.

```
<plugin>
                <artifactId>maven-assembly-plugin</artifactId>
                <version>3.3.0</version>
                <configuration>
                    <archive>
                        <manifest>
                            <mainClass>WordCountFunction</mainClass>
                        </manifest>
                    </archive>
                    <descriptorRefs>
                        <descriptorRef>jar-with-dependencies</
                        descriptorRef>
```

```
            </descriptorRefs>
        </configuration>
        <executions>
            <execution>
                <id>make-assembly</id>
                <phase>package</phase>
                <goals>
                    <goal>single</goal>
                </goals>
            </execution>
        </executions>
    </plugin>
```

The preceding configuration generates jar-with-dependencies when building the project. Let's generate a file using the following command.

```
$./mvnw clean install
```

The Pulsar Functions command-line tool allows you to specify the serializer required. You can now deploy the functions and the serializer using the following command.

```
$ bin/pulsar-admin functions localrun   \
--jar  pulsar-functions/target/pulsar-functions-1.0-SNAPSHOT.jar   \
--classname MovieIngestionFunction \
 --inputs movie-csv-data    \
 --output movie-data    \
 --name movie-reader-v2 \
 --output-serde-classname domain.MovieSrDe
```

This command does the following.

- It configures MovieIngestionFunction to read text data and output Movie objects in Kryo format.

- The --output-side-classname option specifies the serializer fully qualifies the classname.

Send a delimited input message as performed in the previous section. The console consumer prints a binary output instead of JSON text.

The code does not read data in Kryo format. However, if you compose another function that reads this data, you must specify the input de-serializer using the --custom-serde-inputs option.

Pulsar Functions SDK

Pulsar Functions also provides a Java Function Interface that creates functions. The interface provides additional capability to work with a range of features such as state management, message routing, and logging, which are not available in the native language interfaces.

The interface provides a process method that is implemented with user-specified logic. The process method provides data and a context object that provides integration hooks with Pulsar. Using the context, you can perform any of the following tasks.

- Access the logger to trace the output

- Send messages to various topics

- Provide external configuration

- Create monitoring metrics

```
public interface Function<I, O> {
    O process(I input, Context context) throws Exception;
}
```

External Configuration

Passing external configuration is a key feature of the context object. Applications often need this feature to work across different environments. Pulsar allows you to pass configuration by using the user-config property (see Figure 3-4). You can specify a collection of key/value pairs in JSON format. These values are accessible at runtime using the Pulsar Functions SDK.

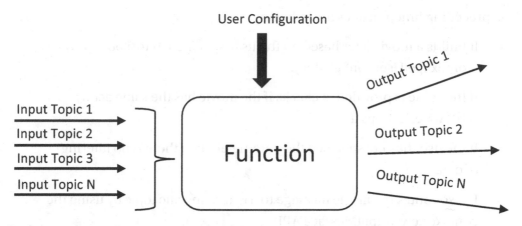

Figure 3-4. *Functions with external configuration*

Continuing the movie data pipeline, you can add a filter to select data based on user-specified actors. Additionally, it can send the movie message to a genre-specific topic. Both these requirements can be implemented using the Context object, as shown next.

```java
public class MovieFilterFunction implements Function<Movie, Movie > {

    @Override
    public Movie process(Movie movie, Context context) throws
    PulsarClientException {
        Optional<Object> actorLookup = context.getUserConfigValue
        ("ActorLookup");
        boolean match = Arrays.stream(movie.getActors()).anyMatch(x ->
                x.equalsIgnoreCase(actorLookup.orElse(x).toString())
        );
        if (!match) {
            return null;
        }
        context.newOutputMessage(movie.getGenre(), Schema.JSON
        (Movie.class))
                    .value(movie)
                    .sendAsync();
        return movie;
    }

}
```

The preceding function does the following.

- It builds a movie filter based on the user-specified ActorLookup value (context.getUserConfigValue).

- If the value is provided, it checks if the movie has the same actor; otherwise, it drops it.

- If the user has not specified the parameter, then there is no filtering of data.

- It also routes the movie message to a genre-specific topic by using the context.newOutputMessage API.

You can now deploy the function along with the --user-config JSON string using the following command.

```
$ bin/pulsar-admin functions localrun    \
--jar  pulsar-functions/target/pulsar-functions-1.0-SNAPSHOT.jar    \
--classname MovieFilterFunction \
 --userConfig { "ActorLookup" : "Eddie Murphy" }\
 --name actor-lookup-data    \
 --inputs movie-data    \
 --output filter-movie
```

Logs

Pulsar Java SDK provides an instance of an SLF4j Logger object that logs information at a specific log level. These generate logs are sent to the function associated log topic (see Figure 3-5) instead of a log file. You can develop function progress monitoring by consuming log messages produced on a log topic.

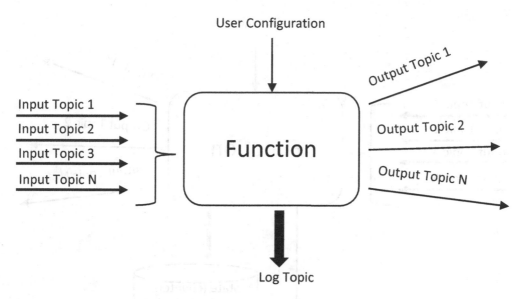

Figure 3-5. *Functions using log topic*

You have used the context.getLogger() in the previously developed MovieFilter example.

```
context.getLogger().info("Processed {} data received from {}", movie,
topicName.orElse("NA"));
```

Pulsar Functions deployment creates a log topic by function name. Optionally, you can also specify the topic to which the log information is produced.

State Storage

The Java SDK provides support to build stateful functions. These functions store application specifies counters and function progress metrics stored in BookKeeper storage. Every function invocation can retrieve the existing data and update it as required (see Figure 3-6). The context object provides necessary APIs like context. putState() and context.getCounter(). Stateful functions have many use cases like average product ratings. The function retrieves existing ratings and total count to compute the newer average rating.

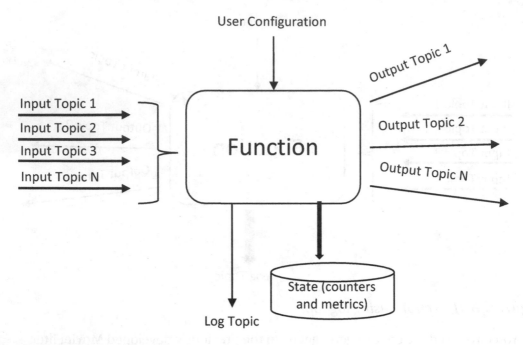

Figure 3-6. *Function state*

Functions CLI provides commands to query the stored data. The capability allows you to use the store for observability needs. The function can track its progress which can be correlated with the count of messages produced.

Testing Functions

Testing is an important aspect of developing software. The practice is applied regardless of the framework or language used. You want to do your best to ensure that you're delivering a quality product.

Pulsar Functions are quite easy to test. Functions created using the language-native support do not need anything else. They can be unit-tested with the framework of your choice, as shown next.

```
public class EncryptFunctionTest {
    @Test
    void shouldTransformText () {
        EncryptFunction encryptFunction = new EcryptFunction();
        String out=ecryptFunction.apply("AttackAtOnce");
```

```
        assertEquals("ExxegoExSrgi",out);
    }
}
```

The preceding code is a unit test for the encrypt function developed at the beginning of the chapter. The unit test is quite simple to write using JUnit. You can instantiate the function and validate the result using assertions.

Testing functions developed using Pulsar SDK is not difficult, using your choice of the unit testing framework. Believing functions consume a few services provided by the context object. You can create mocks to validate the behavior, as shown next.

```
@Test
void shouldGiveBackMovieData() throws PulsarClientException {
        MovieFilterFunction function = new MovieFilterFunction();
        Movie input = new Movie("shrek", "comedy",
                    new String[]{"Eddie Murphy"}, 8);
        Context context = mock(Context.class);
when(context.getUserConfigValue(anyString())).thenReturn(Optional.of
("Eddie Murphy"));
        function.process(input, context);
    verify(context).getUserConfigValue("ActorLookup");
    }
```

Since the Java SerDe interface is quite simple, you can validate an implementation using unit tests and assertions.

Deploying Functions

As discussed earlier, a Pulsar function is deployed to a Pulsar cluster. You must package your function according to the development runtime. Java functions are deployed as a JAR. Files while Python functions are deployed using a Python script. Pulsar runs the deployed functions for every request it receives on the associated topics. Pulsar supports the following modes' functions.

- The local run mode is analogous of the stand-alone setup.

- The Pulsar Functions SDK provides a local runner programmatic API. The cluster mode deploys functions in production environments.

Post-deployment, Pulsar Functions are executed using a runtime provider. The provider is responsible for executing an instance of the deployed Pulsar Function. To maximize deployment flexibility, the Pulsar Functions feature incorporates several execution environments and runtimes listed in Table 3-1.

Table 3-1. *Function Runtimes*

Runtime	Description
Process runtime	Each instance is run as a process. When a function runs in-process mode, it runs on the same machine that the functions worker runs.
Threaded runtime	Each instance is run as a thread. This type applies only to Java instances since the Pulsar Functions framework itself is written in Java. A function runs in thread mode on the same Java virtual machine (JVM) as the functions worker.
Docker runtime	Each instance is run as a Docker container.
Kubernetes runtime	Submit functions as Kubernetes StatefulSet by the functions worker.

Since functions are stateless, you can deploy many instances of a function. By default, Pulsar runs only a single instance of a function. You can change this by specifying parallelism for the deployed function.

LocalRunner

Until now, you have deployed Pulsar Functions locally, thereby launching a runtime and a function in the local run mode. The mode executes the function as a stand-alone application that can be monitored and controlled as a process. Pulsar Functions executed with the local run mode mirror the behavior of execution on a Pulsar cluster.

Programmatic API

Pulsar Functions SDK provides a Programmatic API for deploying functions in local run mode. The API is quite useful in development as you can debug functions using your IDE, specify breakpoints and manually step through the execution.

Note   Programmatic support is only available in Java SDK with Pulsar 2.4 and higher.

```
public class EcryptFunction implements Function<String, String> {

// REMOVED for Brevity

    public static void main(String[] args) throws Exception {
        FunctionConfig functionConfig = new FunctionConfig();
        functionConfig.setName("EcryptMessages");
        functionConfig.setInputs(Collections.singleton("plaintext"));
        functionConfig.setClassName(EcryptFunction.class.getName());
        functionConfig.setRuntime(FunctionConfig.Runtime.JAVA);
        functionConfig.setOutput("ciphertext");
        LocalRunner localRunner = LocalRunner.builder().
        functionConfig(functionConfig).build();
        localRunner.start(true);
    }

}
```

This code block shows the programmatic API parameters in more detail.

- An instance of FunctionConfig is required to configure the function.
- The config provides properties for all command-line options like name, class name, input, and output.
- You must also specify the runtime.
- Additionally, there are properties to configure input and output serializers.

- The config builds a local runner instance.

- The local runner API provides all life cycle methods, like start and stop. Additionally, you can execute these life cycle methods in a non-blocking manner.

Cluster Mode

When you run Pulsar Functions in cluster mode, the code is uploaded to brokers running in a Pulsar cluster. Pulsar distributes the function across the cluster, executes it per the specified runtime mode, and monitors its execution. The mode allows developers to focus on building business required functions without managing their operations. You can submit a function to the cluster using the following command.

```
$ bin/pulsar-admin functions create \
--jar  pulsar-functions/target/pulsar-functions-1.0-SNAPSHOT.jar   \
--classname MovieFilterFunction \
 --userConfig { "ActorLookup" : "Eddie Murphy" }\
 --name actor-lookup-data   \
 --inputs movie-data   \
 --output filter-movie
```

You can trigger a deployed function by using the trigger command. The command is helpful for sanity and smoke testing needs. Triggering a function means that you send a message with a specific value to the function and get the function's output.

```
$ bin/pulsar-admin functions trigger \
--name actor-lookup-data   \
 --topic movie-data   \
 --trigger-value {"name":"shrek", "genre":"comedy", "actors":["Mike
 Myers","Eddie Murphy","Cameron Diaz"], "ratings": 8}
```

Infrastructure-as-code demands keeping all configurations as code. A Pulsar command-line supports option to deploy a function using a YAML-based configuration file. The option is supported for both local and cluster modes.

```
$ bin/pulsar-admin functions create \
 --function-config-file./my-function-config.yaml
```

The Pulsar Functions command-line tool provides various subcommands to support all aspects of function, like listing all deployed functions, updating a function, or checking the state of a function.

Message Delivery Modes

Pulsar Functions allow you to build a data pipeline that can process events as they arise. But there can be failures while processing events. Message processing guarantees allow you to configure a reliability factor for each handled message. Pulsar Functions support the following three distinct messaging guarantees.

- at-most-once

- at-least-once

- effectively-once

By default, Pulsar Functions provide at-most-once delivery guarantees. These guarantees are meaningful because you can always assume the possibility of failures via networks or machines, resulting in data loss. These guarantees enable you to build resilient data pipelines.

At-Most-Once

The at-most-once mode doesn't provide a processing guarantee. No attempts are made to retry or retransmit events if it was lost in transmission, or the function failed to process it (see Figure 3-7). Thus each message is processed once or not at all.

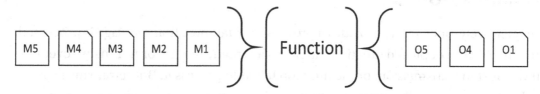

Figure 3-7. Possible data loss

Pulsar Functions configured in at-most-once mode immediately acknowledge a message regardless of its processing. The processing mode is relevant to cases where historical data loss is acceptable and current data is of most value. Stock market data ticks is a possible use case where you are interested in current value rather than any older value.

At-Least-Once

The at-least-once mode guarantees that message is processed by the deployed function. Attempts are made to retry or retransmit events if it was lost in transmission, or the function failed to process it. However, the retransmission can lead to duplicate messages that are processed multiple times (see Figure 3-8), thus the at-least-once mode.

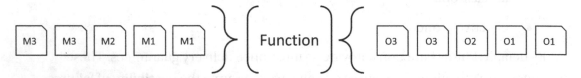

Figure 3-8. *Possible data duplicattion*

Pulsar Functions configured in at-least-once mode read a message from the input topic, execute its logic, and acknowledge the message successfully processed. The processing mode is relevant when data loss is not acceptable, but repeated processing does not alter the validity of data. Data classification is one such use case. You can repeatedly classify movie data based on its rating and genre.

Effectively-Once

The effectively-once mode provides a processing guarantee that message is processed only once by the deployed function. Attempts are made to retry or retransmit events if it was lost in transmission, or the function failed to process it. But retransmission can lead to duplicate messages which are neglected as the message was processed (see Figure 3-9). This method requires that a transaction log be maintained for every processed message

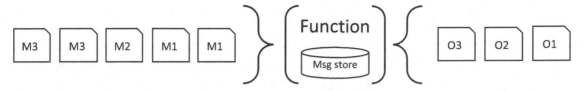

Figure 3-9. *Guarantee single processing*

Pulsar Functions are configured with exactly-once mode function reads the message from the input topic, checks transaction log for a possible duplicate message, then executes its logic. It acknowledges the message post its successful processing or if found duplicate. The function also builds a transaction log of all successfully processed messages. An item order system is a use case for effectively-once processing. You would like to process a message only once; processing is multiple times, which changes the overall quantity, and dropping it cancels the order.

Pulsar deploys functions with the at-least-once mode. You can pass the modes as part of the Pulsar Functions command-line tool, as follows.

```
$ bin/pulsar-admin functions create \
  --configFile ./my-function-config.yaml
```

Summary

This chapter discussed Pulsar Functions for building data pipelines. You looked at the different ways of building function. The language-native approach offered the most vendor-neutral solution, but. As you can see, the language-native approach provides a clean, API-free way of writing functions in Pulsar and is ideal for developing stateless event processors. But it lacks some advanced features like serialization, routing, and logging, which are available in Pulsar Functions SDK. You discussed the various possible deployments and the associated delivery modes. Finally, you built an end-to-end pipeline for the move processing example. In the next chapter, you work with Pulsar Schema Registry to build a uniform message exchange.

## CHAPTER 4

Schema Registry

This chapter outlines using a schema registry in Apache Pulsar.

In traditional approaches, data is transferred using streams of bytes that are interpreted by the receiver. The major problem with using raw bytes is the compatibility and verification of the data that is being transferred. Adding and removing a field in a message can lead to multiple issues. An entire system can have issues when a single field is added or removed when using bytes, which wastes time debugging and fixing.

Information about the structure of data is not present anywhere. The programmer needs to check the binaries of the end systems, which means that they are stuck looking through diffs trying to figure out where things went wrong. There is no single canonical source for making decisions about data structure as it flows through a system.

If the data is structured, you can build pipelines that can adapt as the data changes. Furthermore, the data can be connected to databases, indexes, or analytics tools.

Schema-on-Write vs. Schema-on-Read

Before writing any data, the data types, rows, columns, and other data are defined. The schema is checked when the data is written, and any data that does not conform to the schema throws an error. This approach is called *schema-on-write*.

Another approach is called *schema-on-read*, in which all the messages are stored in unstructured byte arrays. A predefined structure is applied to the data only when the data is being read.

The following are some of the advantages of schema-on-read.

- Different roles and authorization have access to the same shared data, but the type of access and the insights required for one user can differ from another user's. In schema-on-write, all the nuances must be thought through beforehand. The schema is created based on the

© Rahul Sharma and Mohammad Atyab 2022
R. Sharma and M. Atyab, *Cloud-Native Microservices with Apache Pulsar*,
https://doi.org/10.1007/978-1-4842-7839-0_4

requirements. This kind of schema has something for everyone but is not a perfect fit for all users. Practicality diminishes in huge amounts of data.

- With schema-on-read, data can be presented in a schema that adapts best to the queries being issued. You are not stuck with a one-size-fits-all schema. When designing a schema, you can consider all the use cases, but new categories come with time, which requires code changes. With schema-on-read, you are not tied to a predetermined structure. The data can be presented in a schema that is most relevant to the task at hand.

- When multiple data sets are consolidated, more issues creep in. An extensive data modeling job is required with schema-on-write. A bigger and better schema must be rewritten to cover all the data sets that need to be consolidated. Even if the new schema handles everything, more changes will be needed to add, change, or drop a column—or more. With schema-on-read, this upfront modeling exercise disappears.

- The time required to create a schema is saved. The schema-on-read approach means data can be loaded as-is and value is gained right away.

Schema Registry and Pulsar

Let's discuss how to implement schema-on-read. In Pulsar, this is done using the schema registry. Pulsar 2.0 introduced the schema registry to provide a central repository for schema and metadata. It allows all the services to exchange services and flexibly interact. The sharing of schemas between multiple services is also made effortless.

Without needing an external coordination mechanism, the message producers and consumers of Pulsar topics coordinate on the data topic and structure through the Pulsar broker.

All schemas are registered with a central system. Data producers no longer need to include the full schema text with the payload, only the schema ID, resulting in speedier serialization.

Pulsar can parse the data and throw exceptions when the data is not conforming to the registered schema. An exception is thrown if the data is unexpected (e.g., missing data, an unexpected field, or a double value instead of an integer).

Primitive data types can be registered directly, or a more complex data structure can be registered; for example, a class organization with multiple data elements.

```
public class Organization {
    public long id;
    public String name;
    public String domain;
    public static byte[] serialize(Organization org) {
    //removed for brevity
    }

    public static Organization deserialize(byte[]) {
    //removed for brevity
    }
}
```

Without a schema registry, a message is sent as follows.

```
Producer<byte[]> producer = client.newProducer()
        .topic("sample topic")
        .create();
Organization org = new Organization (1, "Sample Org", "sample.com");
byte[] message = serialize(org);
producer.send(message);
```

Schema compatibility and registration is done on Pulsar using the following REST APIs.

1. Update the schema in the broker.

```
Method: POST
URL : {broker-server}/admin/v2/schemas/{tenant}/{namespace}/{topic}/schema
Request Json:
{
    "type": "STRING",
    "schema": "",
```

```
        "properties": {
              "key1": "value1"
        }
}
Response:
200 OK:
{
"version": "1"
}
```

2.   Register the schema.

```
Method: GET
Sample Response:
[{
        "version": 1,
        "type": "STRING",
        "schema": "",
        "timestamp": "1632892450",
        "properties": {
              "key1": "value1"
        }
}]
```

3.   Test the schema's compatibility.

```
Method: POST
URL : {broker-server}/admin/v2/schemas/{tenant}/{namespace}/{topic}/schema
Request Json:
{
        "type": "STRING",
        "schema": "",
        "properties": {
              "key1": "value1"
        }
}
```

```
Response:
{
"schemaCompatibilityStrategy": "string",
"compatibility": true
}
```

Once the schema is registered, all the transferred data mentions the schema version.

Each message is stamped with the name and version of the schema it represents. With data schemas, every single piece of data traveling through the system is completely discoverable, enabling you to build systems that can easily adapt as the payload evolves.

Let's use the example where bytes were sent. You can register the schema in the JSON format.

```
Producer<byte[]> producer = client.newProducer(JSONSchema.
of(Organization.class))
        .topic("sample topic")
        .create();
Organization org = new Organization (1, "Sample Org", "sample.com");
producer.send(org);
```

In the previous example, serialization, deserialization, and type checking were done in the application. Here, this heavy lifting is done by Pulsar.

SchemaInfo

Pulsar schema is defined in a data structure called SchemaInfo.

SchemaInfo is stored and enforced on a per-topic basis and cannot be stored at the namespace or tenant levels. The data sent on one topic can have a different schema than the other, since SchemaInfo storage and enforcement are done at a topic level.

SchemaInfo consists of the following fields.

- **Name**: A schema can have a human-readable name.

- **Type**: This can be either predefined or complex. Pulsar has two complex types: AvroBaseStructSchema and ProtobufNativeSchema.

- **Schema (payload)**: This field contains the actual schema in the form of a JSON string-string map. In a primitive type SchemaInfo, this is a blank string.

- **Properties**: This is a string-string map. Application-specific logic is stored in this map. The objects are registered. The data in the map is purely for application use. The application can use this for various purposes, such as a hash associated with the schema, environment-specific variables, serialization, and deserialization.

The following is a Java example.

```
//removed for brevity
public static SchemaInfo newSchemaInfo(String name, SchemaData data) {
  SchemaInfo si = new SchemaInfo();
  si.setName(name);
  si.setSchema(data.getData());
  si.setType(data.getType());
  si.setProperties(data.getProps());
  return si;
}
```

The following is a timestamp SchemaInfo.

```
{
    "name": "test-string-schema",
    "type": " TIMESTAMP",
    "schema": "",
    "properties": {}
}
```

The type mentioned here can be primitive or complex.

Primitive Data Types

The following are primitive data types.

```
BOOLEAN, INT8, INT16, INT32, INT64, FLOAT, DOUBLE, BYTES, STRING, TIMESTAMP
(DATE, TIME), INSTANT, LOCAL_DATE, LOCAL_TIME, LOCAL_DATE_TIME.
```

These data types are supported in Java. The Python and Go clients do not support all of them. The properties object can be used in primitive data types (e.g., encoding type in a string).

In a primitive data type, a SchemaInfo object is tested as follows.

```java
public class SchemaInfoTest {
    private static final String INT32_SCHEMA_INFO = "{\n"
        + "  \"name\": \"INT32\",\n"
        + "  \"schema\": \"\",\n"
        + "  \"type\": \"INT32\",\n"
        + "  \"properties\": {}\n"
        + "}";
    @Test
    public void testSchemaInfoToString(SchemaInfo si, String jsonifiedStr){
        assertEquals(Schema.STRING.getSchemaInfo(), INT32_SCHEMA_INFO);
    }
```

The following demonstrates the usage of a string schema by a producer and consumer.

```java
// removed for brevity
Producer<String> producer = client.newProducer(Schema.STRING).create();
producer.newMessage().value("Test Data 1").send();
```

```java
//other code removed for brevity
Consumer<String> consumer = client.newConsumer(Schema.STRING).subscribe();
consumer.receive();
```

Complex Data Types

Pulsar supports the following complex data types.

- **Key/value**: A complex key/value pair type can be sent when registering a schema.

- **Struct**: Pulsar supports AvroBaseStructSchema and ProtobufNativeSchema encoding.

Key/Value

Pulsar supports key/value pairs in two ways: inline or separated. When using inline, both key/value pairs are encoded together, and if separated, they are encoded separately.

A key/value pair schema is created as follows.

- Inline: Both the key and the value are encoded together by Pulsar in the message payload. This is used in cases where the key and the value have the same schema or encoding types, like UTF-16.

```
Schema<KeyValue<Integer, String>> kvSchema = Schema.KeyValue(
Schema.INT64,
Schema.STRING,
KeyValueEncodingType.INLINE
);
```

- Separated: The key and value are separated because the key is sent in the message key, whereas the value is encoded in the payload. This is used when the schema for the key and value are different and registered separately. The key can also be used for routing and compaction.

```
Schema<KeyValue<Integer, String>> kvSchema = Schema.KeyValue(
Schema.INT32,
Schema.STRING,
KeyValueEncodingType.SEPARATED
);
```

Once the key/value schema is created, create a producer that produces messages using the schema and consumers that consume the messages.

```
Producer<KeyValue<Integer, String>> producer = client.newProducer(kvSchema)
        .topic(MQ_TOPIC)
        .create();

// send the key/value message
producer.newMessage()
        .value(new KeyValue<>(100, "Test Value"))
        .sequenceId(123)
        .eventTime(System.currentTimeMillis())
        .send();
```

```
//creating a consumer with the same protobuf schema
Consumer<KeyValue<Integer, String>> consumer = client.
newConsumer(kvSchema).topic(MQ_TOPIC)
        .subscriptionName("consumer")
        .subscriptionInitialPosition(SubscriptionInitialPosition.Earliest).
        subscribe();
while (!consumer.hasReachedEndOfTopic()) {
    Message<KeyValue<Integer, String>> msg = consumer.receive();
    KeyValue<Integer, String> kv = msg.getValue();
    System.out.println("got key value : " + kv.getKey() + "\n" +
    kv.getValue());
}
consumer.close();
```

Key/Value Test Cases

Let's look at some test cases to read and write a key/value schema.

The following is for inline.

```
@Test
public void keyValueInlineTest() throws PulsarClientException {
    String topic = "persistent://prop/testnamespace/kv-inline-test";

    @Cleanup
    Producer<KeyValue<String, String>> producer = pulsarClient
            .newProducer(KeyValueSchema.of(Schema.STRING, Schema.STRING))
            .topic(topic)
            .create();

    @Cleanup
    Consumer<KeyValue<String, String>> consumer = pulsarClient
            .newConsumer(KeyValueSchema.of(Schema.STRING, Schema.STRING))
            .topic(topic)
            .subscriptionName("test-subscription")
            .subscribe();
```

```
int numMessage = 10;
for (int i = 0; i < numMessage; i++) {
    producer.newMessage().value(new KeyValue<>(null,
    "testValue")).send();
    producer.newMessage().value(new KeyValue<>("testKey",
    null)).send();
    producer.newMessage().value(new KeyValue<>(null, null)).send();
}

Message<KeyValue<String, String>> message;
KeyValue<String, String> keyValue;
for (int i = 0; i < numMessage; i++) {
    message = consumer.receive();
    keyValue = message.getValue();
    Assert.assertNull(keyValue.getKey());
    Assert.assertEquals("testValue", keyValue.getValue());

    message = consumer.receive();
    keyValue = message.getValue();
    Assert.assertEquals("testKey", keyValue.getKey());
    Assert.assertNull(keyValue.getValue());

    message = consumer.receive();
    keyValue = message.getValue();
    Assert.assertNull(keyValue.getKey());
    Assert.assertNull(keyValue.getValue());
}

}
```

The test cases show how to read and write key/value pairs schema. The key/value map also handles null values.

In the same fashion, the separated encoding can be tested by replacing KeyValueEncodingType.INLINE with KeyValueEncodingType.SEPARATED.

Struct

The next complex type is called a struct. Pulsar supports two struct schemas.

- **AvroBaseStructSchema**: Avro specification is used, which supports AvroSchema, JsonSchema, and ProtobufSchema. The following is an example.

```
@Builder //Lombok notation for creating builder of this //class
@AllArgsConstructor //Lombok notation for creating //constructor that takes
all arguments of this class
@NoArgsConstructor //Lombok notation for creating //constructor that takes
no arguments of this class
public static class Entity {
    String name;
    String domain;
    Date createdAt;
}

Producer<Entity> producer = client.newProducer(Schema.AVRO(Entity.class)).
create();
producer.newMessage().value(Entity.builder()
        .name("test-entity")
        .domain("test-domain.com")
        .createdAt(new Date())
        .build()).send();
```

- **ProtobufNativeSchema**: A protobuf native (version 3) for serialization and deserialization of data. It is used in the following way.

```
public boolean publishMessagesProtobuf(String category, NewsRequest
newsRequest) {
        //use pulsar publish
        String MQ_TOPIC = "persistent://public/default/" + category;
        try {
            PulsarClient client = connectToClient();
            SchemaDefinition def =  SchemaDefinition.<NewsRequest>builder()
```

```java
                .withAlwaysAllowNull(true)
                .withPojo(NewsRequest.class)
                .build();

        //creating a producer with protobuf schema
        Producer<NewsRequest> producer = client.newProducer(Schema.
        PROTOBUF_NATIVE(def)).topic(MQ_TOPIC).create();
        producer.newMessage()
                .value(newsRequest)
                .sequenceId(123)
                .eventTime(System.currentTimeMillis())
                .send();

        producer.close();

        //creating a consumer with the same protobuf schema
        Consumer<NewsRequest> consumer = client.newConsumer(Schema.
        PROTOBUF_NATIVE(def)).topic(MQ_TOPIC)
                .subscriptionName("consumer")
                .subscriptionInitialPosition(SubscriptionInitial
                Position.Earliest).subscribe();
        while (!consumer.hasReachedEndOfTopic()){
            Message<NewsRequest> msg = consumer.receive();
            NewsRequest newsRequestConsumer =  msg.getValue();
            System.out.println("got news message : "+
            newsRequestConsumer.getTitle() + "\n" +
            newsRequestConsumer.getDescription() );
        }
        consumer.close();
        client.close();
    } catch (PulsarClientException e) {
        e.printStackTrace();
        return false;
    }
    return true;
}
```

Auto Schema

When a topic's schema is already registered with a broker, the produced bytes are validated by mentioning AUTO_PRODUCE at the producer end or AUTO_CONSUME at the consumer end. These flags check the compatibility of the message being sent with the schema registered at the broker end.

One example is reading from a Kafka source and producing the same bytes to the Pulsar topic and ensuring whether the bytes can produce Pulsar messages.

```
Produce<byte[]> pulsarProducer = client.newProducer(Schema.AUTO_PRODUCE())
    ...
    .create();
byte[] kafkaMessageBytes = ... ;
pulsarProducer.produce(kafkaMessageBytes);
```

Similarly, a message received at the consumer end can also be sent to another application. You can use AUTO_CONSUME to verify whether the bytes produced by a topic can be sent to the second application. Currently, AUTO_CONSUME supports Avro, JSON, and ProtobufNativeSchema schemas. It deserializes messages into GenericRecord.

```
Consumer<GenericRecord> pulsarConsumer = client.newConsumer(Schema.AUTO_
CONSUME())
    ...
    .subscribe();

Message<GenericRecord> msg = consumer.receive() ;
GenericRecord record = msg.getValue();
```

Schema Version

Each SchemaInfo stored with a topic has a version. The schema version manages changes happening within a topic.

Messages produced with a given SchemaInfo are tagged with a schema version. When a Pulsar client consumes a message, the Pulsar client can use the schema version to retrieve the corresponding SchemaInfo and then use the SchemaInfo to deserialize data.

Schemas are versioned in succession. Schema storage happens in a broker that handles the associated topics so that version assignments can be made.

Once a schema version is assigned, all subsequent messages produced by a producer are tagged with the appropriate version.

Schema Evolution and Compatibility

The registered `SchemaInfo` is stored in an attribute called version. This version lets Pulsar know whether the schema for a topic has been updated.

Schemas store the details of attributes and types. To satisfy new business requirements, you inevitably need to update schemas over time, which is called *schema evolution*.

Any schema changes affect downstream consumers. A schema evolution ensures that the downstream consumers can seamlessly handle data encoded with both old and new schemas.

The schemaRegistryCompatibilityCheckers flag controls most of the compatibility checking. Pulsar supports JSON and Avro compatibility checkers. These can be configured using the following attributes in the broker.

```
"org.apache.pulsar.broker.service.schema.JsonSchemaCompatibilityCheck",
"org.apache.pulsar.broker.service.schema.AvroSchemaCompatibilityCheck"
```

There is one instance of a checker for both schema types.

Whenever a message is sent through a broker (i.e., through a producer, consumer, or a reader), SchemaInfo is also sent to the broker. On receiving the information, the broker initiates the topic schema compatibility checker.

Schema Compatibility Check Strategy

Pulsar provides the strategies listed in Table 4-1.

Table 4-1. *Schema Compatibility Check Strategies*

Compatibility Check Strategy	Changes Allowed	Check Against Which Schemas	Upgrade First
ALWAYS_INCOMPATIBLE	All changes are disabled	All previous versions	None
ALWAYS_COMPATIBLE	All changes are allowed	Compatibility checking disabled	Depends
BACKWARD	Delete fields; Add optional fields	Latest version	Consumers
BACKWARD_TRANSITIVE	Delete fields; Add optional fields	All previous versions	Consumers
FORWARD	Add fields; Delete optional fields	Latest version	Producers
FORWARD_TRANSITIVE	Add fields; Delete optional fields	All previous versions	Producers
FULL	Modify optional fields	Latest version	Any order
FULL_TRANSITIVE	Modify optional fields	All previous versions	Any order

For example, let's take three schemas for topics X, X1, and X2. The schema is updated from X1 to X2 to X3.

ALWAYS_INCOMPATIBLE and ALWAYS_COMPATIBLE are brute-force checkers that either accept all changes or reject all changes in the message format.

If consumers use the latest schema to read messages, backward compatibility makes sure that the messages written with previous schemas are also processed. Using this compatibility, the consumers using the new *X3* schema can process data written by producers using schema X3 or X2, but not necessarily X1; that is, the compatibility is provided for the current and the schema before the current one only. For making all the previous schema compatible (i.e., X3, X2, and X1, BACKWARD_TRANSITIVE can be used).

Suppose there is a consumer that is using the X2 schema. In this compatibility check, it can read the X3 and X2 schemas but not X1. The consumer might not use all the data, but it does not throw an error using a FORWARD check. If there is a requirement to read all the schemas by this consumer, FORWARD_TRANSITIVE can be used.

By using a FULL compatibility check, both forward and backward compatibilities are used. When using FULL_TRANSITIVE, the new schema is forward and backward compatible with all previously registered schemas, not just the last one.

For Avro and JSON, the default schema compatibility check strategy is FULL. For all schema types except Avro and JSON, the default schema compatibility check strategy is ALWAYS_INCOMPATIBLE.

Managing Schemas

The Pulsar schema can be managed either automatically or manually.

Auto Update of Schema: Producer

In cases where there is no schema registered for a producer, the Pulsar broker registers the schema automatically. In other cases, the update happens as shown in Figure 4-1.

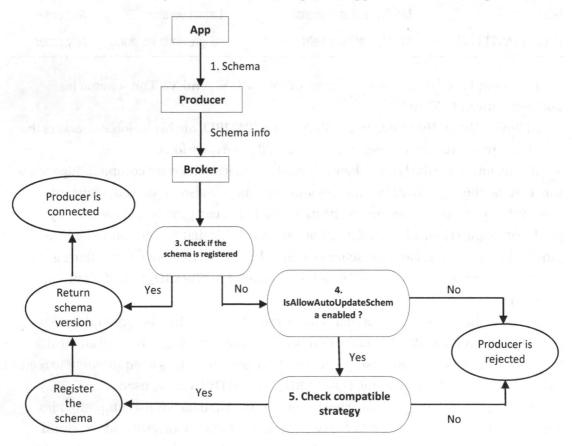

Figure 4-1. *Schema autoupdate flowchart for producers*

Schema AutoUpdate: Consumer

In cases where there is no schema registered for a producer, the Pulsar broker registers the schema automatically. In other cases, the update happens as shown in Figure 4-2.

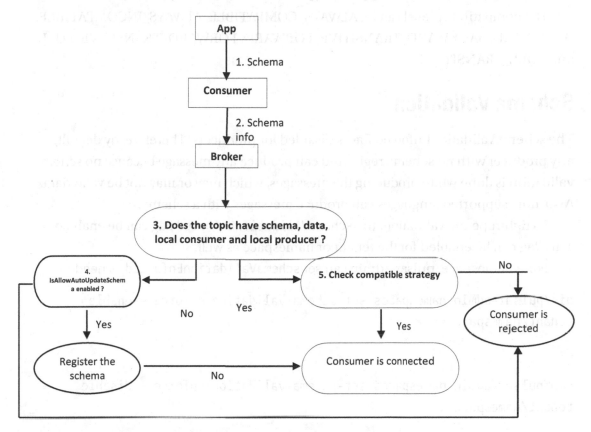

Figure 4-2. *Schema autoupdate for consumers*

Adjust AutoUpdate Strategy

In pulsar-admin, enabling or disabling the auto schema update can be done in the following manner.

```
bin/pulsar-admin namespaces set-is-allow-auto-update-schema --enable
tenant/namespace
```
or
```
bin/pulsar-admin namespaces set-is-allow-auto-update-schema --disable
tenant/namespace
```

For a namespace, `pulsar-admin` can set the schema compatibility strategy as needed.

```
bin/pulsar-admin namespaces set-schema-compatibility-strategy --compatibility
<compatibility-level> tenant/namespace
```

The compatibility level can be ALWAYS_COMPATIBLE, ALWAYS_INCOMPATIBLE, BACKWARD, BACKWARD_TRANSITIVE, FORWARD, FORWARD_TRANSITIVE, FULL, and FULL_TRANSITIVE.

Schema Validation

The schemaValidationEnforced flag is disabled for producers. Therefore, by default, any producer with no schema registered can produce any message because no schema validation is done while producing the messages, which may or may not be valid data. Also, non-supported languages can produce messages with a schema.

To tightrope the validation, the `schemaValidationEnforced` flag can be enabled. This flag can be enabled for the tenant or namespace as well.

For a namespace, pulsar-admin can set `schemaValidationEnforced` as needed.

```
bin/pulsar-admin namespaces set-schema-validation-enforce --enable
tenant/namespace
```

or

```
bin/pulsar-admin namespaces set-schema-validation-enforce --disable
tenant/namespace
```

Manual Schema Management

Pulsar provides CLI tools, the REST API, and Java SDK. This book covers schema management using Java.

To create a schema for Java, PostSchemaPayload is required. It consists of the following fields.

- **Type:** The `schema` type–JSON, Avro, or protobuf.

- **Schema:** UTF-8 encoded string of the schema definition data. In a primitive schema, this array is empty, but in a struct schema, it contains the JSON string of the Avro schema definition.

- **Properties**: The user can supply properties related to this schema. The type of properties is Map<String, String>.

The following is an example of creating a schema from an input file containing schema.

```
public void createSchemaFromFile(String fileName, String type, PulsarAdmin
admin, String ) {
    PostSchemaPayload input = new ObjectMapper().readValue(new
    File(fileName), PostSchemaPayload.class);
    admin.createSchema(topic, input);
}
```

The example takes a file path that the system can read and then creates a schema using that file.

A file's contents may look something like the following.

```
{
    "type": "JSON",
    "schema": "{\"namespace\":\"example.json\",\"type\":\"record\",
    \"name\":\"user\",\"fields\":[{\"name\":\"name\",\"type\":\"string\"},
    {\"name\":\"email\",\"type\":\"string\"},{\"name\":\"salary\",
    \"type\":\"int\",\"default\":\"green\"}]}",
    "properties": {}
}
```

The schema definition in JSON format is saved to a file that can be read, and the schema can be updated.

Getting a Schema

The latest schema can be fetched from the admin using the getSchemaInfo API. If a version is not provided, the latest schema registered is returned; otherwise, the schema of the required version is returned.

```
admin.getSchemaInfo(topic)
```

or

```
admin.getSchemaInfo(topic, version)
```

Deleting a Schema

To delete a schema, simply call the deleteSchema method.

```
admin.deleteSchema(topic);
```

Custom Schema Storage

Apache BookKeeper is the default schema storage used in Pulsar. However, a custom schema storage can be created and deployed on a broker. The interface uses the SchemaStorage and SchemaStorageFactory classes.

```
public interface SchemaStorage {
    // How schemas are updated
    CompletableFuture<SchemaVersion> put(String key, byte[] value,
    byte[] hash);

    // How schemas are fetched from storage
    CompletableFuture<StoredSchema> get(String key, SchemaVersion version);

    // How schemas are deleted
    CompletableFuture<SchemaVersion> delete(String key);

    // Utility method for converting a schema version byte array to a
    SchemaVersion object
    SchemaVersion versionFromBytes(byte[] version);

    // Startup behavior for the schema storage client
    void start() throws Exception;

    // Shutdown behavior for the schema storage client
    void close() throws Exception;
}

public interface SchemaStorageFactory {
    @NotNull
    SchemaStorage create(PulsarService pulsar) throws Exception;
}
```

Deploying the Classes Created

TO deploy the class created, a package in a JAR file needs to be created and uploaded in the lib folder of the installed Pulsar instance. Once this is done, you need to update broker.conf by changing the schemaRegistryStorageClassName field with the newly created class name. Afterward, Pulsar needs to be restarted.

Summary

Pulsar has a built-in mechanism to validate the topic data being sent and received. Schema registry and evolution strategies provide users greater flexibility. Pulsar supports multiple strategies, and it is very easy to use. Out of the box, Pulsar supports JSON and Avro schemas. And with the SchemaStorage interface, it becomes customizable and can be extended for uses not internally provided by Pulsar.

CHAPTER 5

Building Microservices Using Pulsar

Microservice architecture is designed to tackle the complexities of modern large-scale enterprise applications. It employs the "divide and conquer" principle to break down a complex business into smaller services, with complete autonomy of its technology stack. Typically, one microservice can exist alone, but it cannot fulfill business goals alone. Several microservices work together to fulfill the required business goals. A microservice needs to exchange data or trigger other microservices to perform a subtask.

In a microservice architecture, one of the most challenging design decisions involves the way services communicate and share data. The synchronous REST API is the easiest and most common way to communicate between microservices, which is often a pragmatic solution. But the synchronous approach also leads to challenges related to system availability, failure cascading, latency propagation.

Alternatively, microservices can communicate asynchronously using a lightweight broker. The broker is an extension of the SOA concept but with the principle of *smart endpoint and dumb pipes*. The lightweight message broker found in this topology does not perform any orchestration, transformation, or complex routing. Rather, it is a transport facilitating access to remote services. There are several benefits of this topology, including decoupling for scalability and availability, system and load monitoring, and system resilience.

In practice, microservice architecture demands both mechanisms. Synchronous request-response calls are required when the user expects an immediate response. Background behaviors can be achieved using integration patterns based on events and asynchronous messaging, thus providing maximum scalability and resiliency. Some of the world's most scalable architectures, such as LinkedIn and Netflix, use event-driven, asynchronous messaging.

© Rahul Sharma and Mohammad Atyab 2022
R. Sharma and M. Atyab, *Cloud-Native Microservices with Apache Pulsar*,
https://doi.org/10.1007/978-1-4842-7839-0_5

Apache Pulsar provides support for building event-based microservices. In this chapter, you work with various features which can enforce microservice design practices. By the end of the chapter, you can be confident of leveraging Pulsar for asynchronous message-based microservice architecture.

Scenario: Portfolio Tracker

WizKap Inc, a fictional company, is building a portfolio tracker app. The mobile app must capture daily changes in the valuation of financial instruments like stocks and bonds owned by a user. Additionally, it must also show the historical growth in portfolio valuation over the last decade. For simplicity, users can't buy or sell stocks from the app. They can simply change the stocks owned by them on a particular date. The user can also schedule periodic (daily, weekly, monthly) notifications of a summary of the valuations.

The portfolio tracking solution consists of several microservices (see Figure 5-1). Each of these services performs behaviors as outlined next. These services are intended to reflect communication challenges in real-world scenarios.

- **Account service**: Performs management of user accounts. It consists of several use cases like user signup, change password, and user profile lookup.

- **Dashboard service**: Performs portfolio data analysis and computes interactive dashboards, charts using stock-based filters and shows the valuation of user data.

- **Portfolio service**: Keeps track of user portfolio and records the change in its valuation.

- **Ingestion service**: Load valuation of different stocks and bonds. For simplicity, the service loads data from CSV files provided at day end.

- **Price calculator**: There are several instances of the pricing calculator based on instrument type. The approach enables you to perform different price computations for different market instruments, such as bonds and stocks.

- **Scheduler service**: Dispatches requests and manages business workflows. The service triggers periodic notifications.

- **Notification services**: Sends out user notifications as per the configured period.

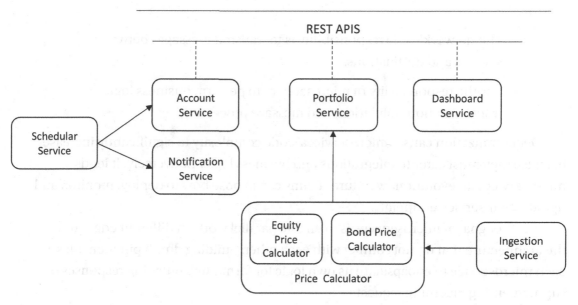

Figure 5-1. *WizKap services*

Account, portfolio, and dashboard services have synchronous REST APIs as they are responsible for handling interactive user requests. On the other hand, the ingestion, price, and portfolio services have an asynchronous event-based communication. Interservice communication allows you to work with Apache Pulsar's features that are aimed at microservices.

Enterprise Integration

Microservices architectural style results in distributed systems, with services that require services to interact over a network. Microservices offer the ability to scale, implement, and evolve services independently, so this communication must be loosely coupled and reliable. This requirement readily fits with the messaging concept, which provides a framework for integrating independent system components or building a set of loosely coupled systems that operate individually, scale, and evolve without interfering with each other.

Microservices design aims to deliver business agility and ownership by replacing the centralized enterprise integration teams, as in SOA, with a decentralized approach. The architecture recommends interservice communication using the principle of *smart endpoints and dumb pipes,* meaning that each service has to take care of all the application integration. The principle segments the responsibility of communications as follows.

- The network's sole responsibility is to transmit messages between sources and destinations.

- It is the responsibility of microservices to perform business logic, transformation, validation, and message processing.

Decentralization causes microservices' code complexity to significantly increase because they must cater to integrations and business logic. Conversely, it lends microservices an evolutionary nature. Teams can choose how to deploy, monitor, and update their service endpoints.

Another goal of microservices is to enable parallel work on different edges of the architecture that do not conflict with each other. Building dumb pipes enables each microservice to encapsulate its own logic for formatting outgoing responses or supplementing incoming requests.

Robust system integration is often performed by following guidelines and practices known as *enterprise integration patterns*. These patterns could be implemented to support the invocation of an arbitrary number of other services. Apache Pulsar clients and functions provide support to implement these patterns. In the following sections, you build an understanding of the fundamental patterns.

Fan-out

The term *fan-out* refers to a messaging design in which a message published by a particular publisher is consumed by multiple subscribers simultaneously and independently (see Figure 5-2). The same message is consumed by different consumers and processed in different ways. The fan-out pattern can be applied where a publisher needs to asynchronously communicate with multiple consumers on the same workload.

The WizKap Inc portfolio tracker solutions have an Ingestion service, which read details from CSV file and publish it to a *day-end-price* topic. The topic has the following two subscribers.

- **EquityPriceCalculator**: Copies the market price as the stock closing price.

- **BondPriceCalculator**: Bond valuation depends on its market value as well as its fixed rate of return. On getting the market price of a Bond, the service load bond details to compute a value based on the rate of return.

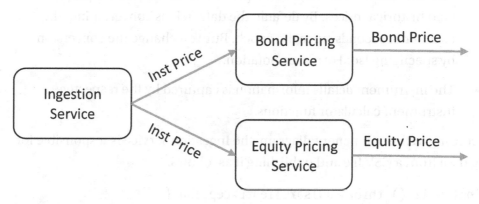

Figure 5-2. *Fan-out data*

Apache Pulsar allows you to create a fan-out subscription using exclusive mode. Chapter 2 covers details around how to achieve the same. Additionally, you must control the message based on the various supported Schema Types. Pulsar has excellent support for JSON-based serialization.

WizKap solution needs to exchange instrument data using the following entity.

```java
public class InstrumentClosePrice {
    private String instrumentId;
    private InstrumentType type;
    private double price;
    @JsonFormat(shape = JsonFormat.Shape.STRING, pattern = "yyyy-MM-dd")
    private Date day;
    private InstrumentDetails details;
}
```

The code describes the InstrumentClosePrice POJO class for sharing market price information.

- The instrumentId specifies the market identifier (e.g., HDFC, GOOGL, SBI, etc.).

- The InstrumentType specifies if the type of the instruments. The system supports bonds and equity types.

- The price specifics the closing price of the instrument.

- The day specified the date of the price. The day is quite helpful to load historical prices. By default, the date field is converter into the number of seconds since the epoch. But You change the conversion by specifying JsonFormat annotation.

- The instrument details information is captured by the respective instrument calculator functions.

According to the component diagram, the Ingestion service is responsible for loading data from a CSV file and publishing it as follows.

```java
void initialize() throws PulsarClientException {
    // Truncated for Brevity
        dayEndPriceProducer = client.newProducer(JSONSchema.
        of(InstrumentClosePrice.class)
                .topic("day-end-price")
                .create();
    }

void readData(String fileLocation) throws Exception {

// Truncated FOR BREVITY

                String[] values = line.split(",");
                InstrumentClosePrice instClosePrice = InstrumentClosePrice.
                builder()
                        .instrumentId(values[1])
                        .type(values[2]))
                        .price(Double.valueOf(values[3]))
                        .day(dateFormat.parse(values[0]))
                        .build();
```

```
        dayEndPriceProducer.send(instClosePrice);
        }
    }
}
```

The following things are handled in the code.

- The initialize method creates a JSON-based schema for the day-end-price topic.

- The read data method reads a CSV file line by line and create InstrumentClosePrice objects.

- Messages are generated using instances of the InstrumentClosePrice POJO class.

On the other end, EquityPriceCalculator and BondPriceCalculator are created as Pulsar functions using native-language support, as follows.

```
class BondPriceFunction implements Function<InstrumentClosePrice,
InstrumentClosePrice> {
// REMOVED FOR BREVITY
if(InstrumentType.Bond.equals(instrumentClosePrice.getType())) {
        BondInstrumentDetail bondInstrumentDetail =
        BondInstrumentDetail.builder()
                .couponRate(10)
                .cumalativePrice(instrumentClosePrice.getPrice())
                .build();

 // create bondClosePrice
        }
 retrun   bondClosePrice;
}
```

This function determines the required BondInstrumentDetail and enriches the InstrumentClosePrice with the information. It is important to note that BondInstrumentDetail and EquityInstrumentDetail are implementations of the InstrumentDetail interface. Both price calculator functions are deployed as separate subscriptions using the following command.

```
./bin/pulsar-admin functions localrun
 --jar priceCalculator/target/PriceCalculator-1.0-SNAPSHOT-jar-with-
dependencies.jar \
 --classname BondPriceCalculator \
 --name bond-calculator  \
 --inputs day-end-price  \
 --schema-type json \
 --output bond-day-end-price
```

Fan-in

The fan-in pattern is a method to consolidate the data coming from different sources and send processed data to another place. You can think about it as like reduction because multiple events are aggregated in fewer ones. The consolidation process generally takes place within the component that captures the different events (see Figure 5-3). Application of the fan-in pattern helps develop a simple data processing solution and keeps resource utilization to a minimum.

The WizKap Inc. portfolio tracker solution is responsible for aggregating the prices published by EquityPriceCalcutor and BondPriceCalculator. These prices must calculate valuations for every user.

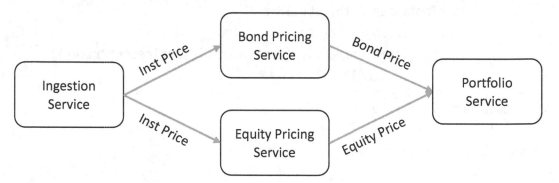

Figure 5-3. *Portfolio fan-in service*

Apache Pulsar allows you to create a fan-in consumer by subscribing to multiple topics. This way, the consumer is delivered all messages, which are aggregated as per the business logic. Please make sure that all topics support the same schema; otherwise, there may be issues related to message conversion. The portfolio service is responsible for consuming and aggregating as follows.

```java
void initialize() throws PulsarClientException {

    // Truncated for Brevity

    dayEndPriceConsumer = client.newConsumer(JSONSchema.
    of(InstrumentClosePrice.class)
            .topic("bond-day-end-price","eq-day-end-price"))
            .subscriptionName("portfolio-update")
            .build())
            .subscribe();
}

void readData() throws IOException {
    while (true) {
        Message<InstrumentClosePrice> msg = dayEndPriceConsumer.
        receive();
        InstrumentClosePrice value = msg.getValue();

        // Truncated For Brevity

        dayEndPriceConsumer.acknowledge(msg);
    }
}
```

The following are performed in the code.

1. The initialize method creates a consumer on multiple topics using JSON-based schema.

2. The read data method waits for the InstrumentClosePrice message from the topic.

3. It then validates the type of instrument and updates user valuations accordingly.

4. It sends an acknowledgment to mark the successful processing of the message.

This fan-in pattern is applicable for different use cases. It aggregates the data from different sources. It can also support window-based aggregations in use cases with a high volume of events. This pattern can be extended to create a single event from multiple events of the same data source that fall within a particular range, such as a time interval. Rather than aggregating the pattern, it can also queue events arriving from different sources to support priority-based executions.

Router

Routing is the concept that enables a producer to send messages to an underlying channel and then leave it to the integration provider to deliver it to the required consumers. The concept primarily decouples the source from the intended consumers. Pulsar provides topics for message routing, which is covered in Chapter 2.

While working with topics is easy, but there can be several scenarios that might ask for a relook at the integration approach. Applications can produce a topic, irrespective of who is their consumer. At times this may lead to topics containing uber data. In such cases, downstream services may not need all the messages published on this topic. Thus, there is a challenge on how to support these use cases. The following choices help downstream services perform efficiently.

- Consumers can filter out the non-required messages. The approach recommends building filters using Pulsar functions, matching messages based on their content and dropping the non-matching ones. The function enables you to build a data pipeline that can transform and enrich the original message. Please refer to Chapter 3 for more information.

- Producers can produce on different topics, utilizing the fan-out pattern.

Interservice Communication

Microservices must communicate efficiently and reliably. This can be difficult when multiple services work together to complete a business process. Each service needs commodity features that are not a part of the core business logic, such as resilient communication, transport-level security, and observability. Implementing these in each microservice is overwhelmingly complex. The effort required could greatly increase if the microservices are written in multiple (polyglot) languages.

The following section presents some of the main challenges arising from service-to-service communication. You also look at ways to address these concerns using Apache Pulsar.

Resiliency

Each microservice may have many deployed instances. However, an instance can fail for a variety of reasons. There can be a hardware failure or a VM reboot, or an instance might crash or overburden and not be able to process new requests. Each of these situations would result in an invocation failure. Thus microservice must be designed to encounter, identify, and handle failure as gracefully as possible. Apache Pulsar provides dead-letter queues and retries that can make service-to-service network calls more resilient.

Dead-Letter Queues

A variety of possible issues can lead to messages not being processed. For example, incorrect conditions within the producer or consumer application or an unexpected state change can cause problems with your application. The purpose of the dead-letter queue is to hold messages that can't be delivered to any receiver or messages that cannot be processed (see Figure 5-4). Services can then fix issues and resubmit the messages from the DLQ. A DLQ should allow listing for viewing the contents of the queue, purging for clearing those contents and merging for reprocessing the dead-lettered messages, allowing comprehensive resolution for all failures affected by a shared issue

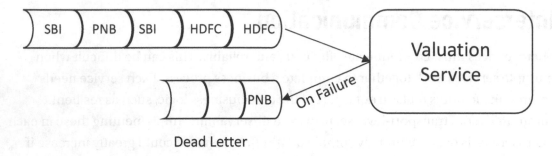

Dead Letter

Figure 5-4. *Dead-letter queues*

Pulsar would attempt to redeliver the message which had failed with negative acknowledgment or timeout. When the delivery count exceeds the limit, the message is moved to the DLQ.

The valuation service is responsible consuming and aggregating prices. It can be enhanced to handle failed messages using dead-letter queue as follows.

```
void initialize() throws PulsarClientException {
       dayEndPriceConsumer = client.newConsumer(JSONSchema.
       of(InstrumentClosePrice.class))
               .topic("bond-day-end-price","eq-day-end-price")
               .subscriptionName("portfolio-update")
               .subscriptionType(SubscriptionType.Shared)
               .ackTimeout(5, TimeUnit.SECONDS)
               .deadLetterPolicy(DeadLetterPolicy.builder()
                       .maxRedeliverCount(3)
                       .deadLetterTopic("failed-day-end-price")
                       .build())
               .subscribe();
   }
void readData() throws IOException {
       while (true) {
           Message<InstrumentClosePrice> msg = dayEndPriceConsumer.
           receive();
           try {
               InstrumentClosePrice value = msg.getValue();

               // Truncated for Brevity
```

```
        dayEndPriceConsumer.acknowledge(msg);

    } catch (Exception e) {
        dayEndPriceConsumer.negativeAcknowledge(msg);
    }
  }
}
```

The following are handled in the code.

- The initialize method creates a consumer on multiple topics using JSON-based schema.

- The subscription is enabled with the dead-letter topic configuration. You can specify the dead-letter topic name; otherwise, Pulsar would suffix the topic with *DLQ*.

- You can also specify the redelivery count, after which the message is sent to the DLQ topic.

- The read data method waits for the InstrumentClosePrice message class and then updates user valuations.

- Sends acknowledgment to mark successful processing of the message. But on failure, it sends back a negative acknowledgment.

The subscription also allows configuring acknowledgment timeouts, which can also enforce redelivery. It is often recommended to prefer negative acknowledgments over timeouts as the practice yield better throughput by avoiding idle time.

Note   The dead-letter topic is enabled only in the shared subscription mode. You cannot use it with exclusive and failover subscription modes.

A dead-letter queue is primarily responsible for handling failed messages. It is a way to set aside and isolate messages that cannot be processed properly so that you can proceed unblocked. Deadhead queues let you achieve the following goals.

- Easy debugging of an errored message's workflow

- Configure notifications and alerts for dead-letter messages

- Review logs to determine whether exceptions led to message deliveries to dead-letter queues

- Examine messages in a dead-letter queue to diagnose content related issues

- Determine if the consumer has enough time to process messages

Retries

An invocation may fail because of a transient fault that goes away by itself. Rather than fail outright, the subscriber can retry the message processing a certain number of times. But the retry operation can lead to performance challenges in a high-volume system. The failed message can clog the service processing as it does not allow to pick new messages.

Apache Pulsar addresses the problem of retries by enabling a distinct retry queue for every subscription. When a consumer handler returns a failed response for a given message after a certain number of retries, the consumer publishes that message to its corresponding retry topic (see Figure 5-5). However, the service business logic must provide idempotent processing of the messages. Retries can cause unintended side effects if the processing is not idempotent.

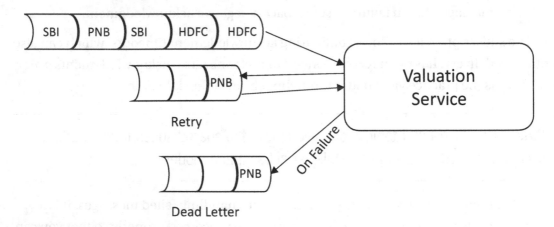

Figure 5-5. *Retry queues*

The valuation service is responsible for consuming and aggregating prices. It can be enhanced to handle failed messages using retries as follows.

```
void initialize() throws PulsarClientException {
        dayEndPriceConsumer = client.newConsumer(JSONSchema.
        of(InstrumentClosePrice.class))
            .topic("bond-day-end-price","eq-day-end-price")
            .subscriptionName("portfolio-update")
            .enableRetry(true)
            .subscriptionType(SubscriptionType.Shared)
            .deadLetterPolicy(DeadLetterPolicy.builder()
                    .maxRedeliverCount(3)
                    .retryLetterTopic("retry-day-end-price")
                    .deadLetterTopic("failed-day-end-price")
                    .build())
            .subscribe();
}

void readData() throws IOException {
        while (true) {
            Message<InstrumentClosePrice> msg = dayEndPriceConsumer.
            receive();
            try {
                InstrumentClosePrice value = msg.getValue();

                // Truncated for Brevity

                dayEndPriceConsumer.acknowledge(msg);
                }
            } catch (Exception e) {
                dayEndPriceConsumer.reconsumeLater(msg, 2*(msg.
                getRedeliveryCount()+1), TimeUnit.MINUTES);
            }
        }
    }
```

The following are performed in the code.

- The initialize method creates a consumer on multiple topics using JSON-based schema.

- The subscription is enabled with a dead-letter configuration. You can specify the dead-letter topic name; otherwise, Pulsar would suffix the topic with *DLQ*.

- You must enable the retry property of the subscription and optionally provide the retry topic name.

- You can also specify the redelivery count, after which the message is sent to the DLQ topic.

- The read data method waits for the InstrumentClosePrice message class and then updates user valuations.

- Sends acknowledgment to mark successful processing of the message. But on failure, it rejects the message with the reconsumeLater API instead of negative acknowledgment.

- reconsumeLater allows you to specify an exponential backoff period by using the retry count available in the message.

Throttling

Typically, the load on an application depends on the number of active users and the types of workflows they perform. For example, B2B systems are likely to have more active users during business hours, or there can be computationally expensive analysis and reporting at the end of each month. On the other hand, B2C systems might have unanticipated bursts of activity caused due to varying circumstances, such as economic outlook, political change, and so forth. The system suffers poor performance and may even fail if the processing requirements exceed the capacity of the available resources. With the software-as-a-service model, a service is often backed with a service-level agreement, and failing to meet the agreement could lead to unacceptable financial losses. Even in B2C applications, such downtimes lead to reputation loss and customer backlash.

Throttling is the practice of limiting the number of active requests to a service from each user. The threshold is important to protect limited resources from a surge of processing. Sometimes, a small number of users creates an excessive load. This can have an impact on other users and can reduce the overall availability of your application. When a single client makes excessive requests, the application might throttle the client for a certain period. The practice can reduce this risk from accidental or malicious overloads. During the throttling period, the application refuses some or all of the requests from that client. Throttling comes in two forms.

- **Publisher throttling**: The maximum rate of messages published for a producer must be less than the infrastructure capacity.

- **Subscriber throttling**: Defines the throughput for the service— that is, the maximum rate of messages it can respond to, otherwise known as a *service-level agreement* (SLA). Additionally, consumer throttling ensures that consumers access the infrastructure as per the configured limits.

Note   Apache Pulsar allows to build throttling limits using namespaces and tenants. The WizKap application is deployed in the default namespace of the public tenant, which is not recommended practice. The solution would still allow you to enable limits, but it is better to organize them in different namespaces while working in enterprise applications.

To be effective, throttling must be performed quickly. Pulsar can detect an increase in activity and react accordingly. It is also able to return quickly to its original state after the load has eased. The *topicPublisherThrottlingTickTimeMillis* parameter in broker.conf allows you to configure the time for evaluating the throttling rate.

Publisher Throttling

Publisher throttling is commonly used to protect services by managing the incoming traffic to each service. This is accomplished on a topic source basis. Throttling Publishers can be extremely useful when there has been an abnormally high level of traffic on a particular topic (see Figure 5-6). In such scenarios, throttling the producer that feeds the topic allows its consumers to catch up while still servicing other users. Without throttling, a single publisher could consume all of the available capacity to the detriment of other users. Additionally, no tracking information is available to help future size requirements for the service.

In the WizKap app, the ingestion service is publishing messages to its consumers. You can limit the service rate so that it does not run then BondPriceCalculator and EquityPriceCalculator consumers.

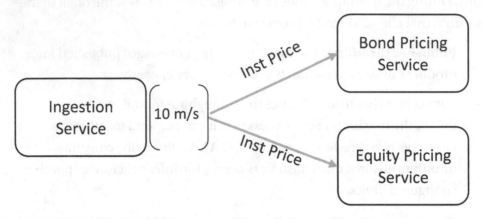

Figure 5-6. *Producer throttling*

```
./bin/pulsar-admin namespaces set-publish-rate -m 10 public/default
```

This command configures the following behavior.

- Set the rate as 10 messages/sec. Optionally you can also limit the size of bytes published

- Specifies the *public* tenant and *default* namespace

The command would set the rate for all topics in the namespace, impacting the other producers publishing to other topics in the same namespace. pulsar-admin also provides a command to read the limits. You can also remove the limits by issuing the following command.

```
./pulsar-admin namespaces remove-publish-rate public/default
```

Subscriber Throttling

There are several reasons for using subscriber rate limits. First, a service can use it to protect itself from any kind of overruns without investing in a commodity requirement. It also defines the SLA for the consumer as it can't respond to the topic more than the required rate (see Figure 5-7). In a shared subscription, the limits make sure that a fast consumer does not process all published messages and thus provides message distribution.

In the WizKap app, the Ingestion service is publishing messages to its consumers. You can safeguard the behavior of BondPriceCalculator and EquityPriceCalculator consumers by adding subscriber rates so they can perform in agreed bounds.

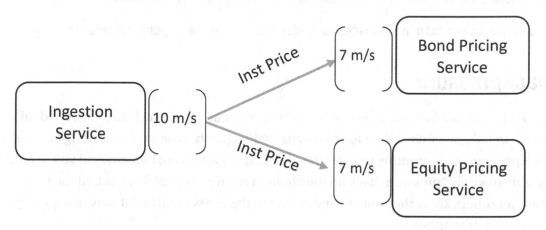

Figure 5-7. *Subscriber throttling*

```
./bin/pulsar-admin namespaces set-subscribe-rate -m 1 public/default
```

This command specifies the following.

- The *public* tenant and *default* namespace
- Sets the rate as 7 messages/second; optionally, you can also limit the size of bytes published

The command would set a rate for all topics in the namespace, impacting the other producers publishing to other topics in the same namespace. pulsar-admin also provides a command to read the limits. You can also remove the limits by issuing the following command.

```
./bin/pulsar-admin namespaces remove-subscribe-rate public/default
```

Dispatch Throttling

Apache Pulsar Producers and subscribers can perform well at a very high volume of message exchanges. The high volume of messages on a particular topic can have adverse effects on other topics. The exchange consumes most of the available resources, thus leading to degraded performance for other clients. Pulsar provides dispatch rate-limiting to guard against these scenarios and to support a fair utilization of resources.

Dispatch throttling allows you to exchange only the configured number of messages to the consumers/publishers regardless current publish rate or backlog on that topic. Similar to other mechanisms, it can be restricted by the number of messages per second (msg-dispatch-rate) or by the number of bytes of messages per second.

```
./bin/pulsar-admin namespaces set-dipatch-rate -m 1 public/default
```

Backpressure

Backpressure is a key characteristic of microservices architecture. It allows individual nodes to fail gracefully if their load exceeds their capacity instead of cascading failures. Backpressure in computing terms is the idea that resources are limited. And you should be able to apply "pressure" back up the chain to relieve some of that load. At the very least, let others know that you are under load in the ecosystem, and it may take time to process their requests.

There are a variety of strategies with which you can exercise flow control and backpressure to alleviate the problems caused when a quickly-producing producer meets a slow-consuming subscriber. Almost universally, you are talking about a way to tell anyone trying to add more items in the queue that either they simply cannot enqueue any more items or that they need to back off for a period of time. Alternatively, you are talking about queues purely dropping messages once a certain capacity is reached.

Backlog Quotas

Apache Pulsar keeps track of all messages received on subscriptions. Once a message is acknowledged, then Pulsar deletes it, as it is no longer required. On the other hand, all unacknowledged messages are retained by Pulsar in a backlog. Since a topic can have multiple subscriptions, a message must be acknowledged in all subscriptions before Pulsar can consider it ready for deletion.

But disk storage has limits, and messages can't be stored forever while Pulsar waits for a consumer to acknowledge them. In fast publisher and slow consumer scenarios, subscription backlogs can be controlled by enabling backlog quotas. Once the quota is reached, there are a few options to handle the processing. Pulsar provides the following message retention policies to handle backlog quota overruns.

- **producer_request_hold**: The broker holds and does not persist the producer message. Pulsar holds the producer's send request until the backlog has room for more messages or it times out.

- **producer_exception**: The broker disconnects the client by throwing a ResourceAllocation exception, signaling that the buffer is full.

- **consumer_backlog_eviction**: If an overflow happens, the oldest message is simply ignored, and only the new values are delivered once the downstream consumer requests.

The backlog quota applies per topic and is defined by the following parameters of the broker.conf file.

- The backlogQuotaCheckEnabled parameter toggles the backlog check for all topics.

- The backlogQuotaCheckIntervalInSeconds defines the time interval for scheduling the check.

- The backlogQuotaDefaultLimitGB parameter sets a limit on the maximum backlog size permitted for the topic.

- The backlogQuotaDefaultRetentionPolicy parameter configures the policy for handling the check.

Since a topic can have multiple backlogs, Pulsar applies the limit to the largest subscription backlog (i.e., from the slowest consumer).

In the WizKap app, the schedular service runs daily and weekly schedules for notifications. It invokes the account service and then sends a message to the notification service, which creates a message and sends it out since the notification service is interacting with external services to enforce backlog. Quats to manage backpressure. You can also fine-tune backlog quota for individual topics by using the following pulsar-admin command.

```
./bin/pulsar-admin namespaces set-backlog-quota my-tenant/my-ns  --limit
2G  --policy producer_exception
```

This command configures the following behaviors.

- Specifies the *public* tenant and *default* namespace

- Sets the limit of 2 GB of all messages

Note   The default broker option is producer_request_hold. It is the least intrusive option because it relies on consumers to drain the backlog.

The command would set a rate for all topics in the namespace, impacting the other producers publishing to other topics in the same namespace. pulsar-admin also provides a command to read the limits. You can also remove the limits by issuing the following command.

```
./bin/pulsar-admin namespaces remove-backlog-quota public/default
```

Time-to-Live (TTL)

Pulsar stores all unacknowledged messages forever. It also supports a time-to-live (TTL) parameter to manage these unacknowledged messages. The parameter refers to the amount of time an unacknowledged message is set to exist before being discarded by Pulsar, thereby freeing up the disk space.

Pulsar allows you to specify the TTL for all topics using the *ttlDurationDefaultInSeconds* parameter in broker.conf. Optionally, you can configure TTL parameters for the required topics using the following pulsar-admin command.

```
./bin/pulsar-admin namespaces set-message-ttl public/
default  --messageTTL 120
```

This command configures the following behavior.

- Specifies the *public* tenant and *default* namespace

- Sets a limit of 120 seconds or 2 minutes for each unacknowledged message

The command would set a rate for all topics in the namespace, impacting the other producers publishing to other topics in the same namespace. pulsar-admin also provides a command to read the limits. You can also remove the limits by issuing the following command.

```
./bin/pulsar-admin namespaces remove-message-ttl public/default
```

Note   You can only use the TTL parameter if you can discard messages without incurring a data loss. In the current WizKap app, there are no business flows that can leverage this safely.

Topic Compaction

Topic compaction is the process of reading through the backlog of the topic and retaining only the latest message for each key in a compacted backlog. The compaction is non-destructive, and consumers can control to read compacted or the non-compacted data. There are several use cases of compacted data like cached data, steaming data.

Topic compaction is a granular retention mechanism that retains the last update for each key. A compacted topic log contains a full snapshot of final record values for every record key, not just the recently changed keys (see Figure 5-8).

In the WizKap app, there is a future requirement of showing real-time portfolio valuations. The ingestion service which loads the data at day intervals is not good enough, and thus the real-time data is fetched using NSE market streams. It provides the same data, but there are frequent updates. These updates trigger valuation computations, but there is a time value attached with each unacknowledged message. The value diminishes as soon as there is a new message for the same market instrument. There is no value in generating valuations based on stale data. This is an appropriate use-case of topic compaction.

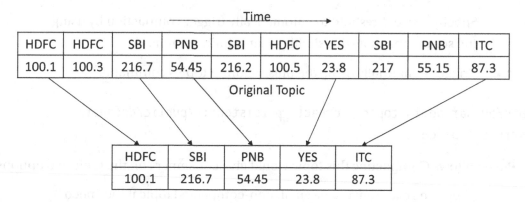

Figure 5-8. *Compaction*

To use topic compaction, you have to make sure that keys are the same for the required messages. You can create an InstrumentUpdate service with the following code.

```
// Truncated for Brevity
void process(String update) throws Exception {

                String[] values = line.split(",");
                InstrumentUpdate instUpdate = InstrumentUpdate.builder()
                        .instrumentId(values[1])
                        .price(Double.valueOf(values[3]))
                        .day(dateFormat.parse(values[0]))
                        .build();
                dayEndPriceProducer.newMessage()
                        .value(instUpdate)
                        .key(instUpdate.getInstrumentId())
                        .send();
        }
```

The following is performed in the code.

- Invokes the newMessage method to build a TypedMessage that allows specifying keys

- Specifies the instrument ID as the message key

Next, you must trigger the process of compaction on the Pulsar broker. The process must be invoked at periodic intervals by following either of the following ways.

- Specify a size threshold to automatically trigger compaction by using the set-compaction-threshold pulsar-admin command.

- Trigger it manually using the pulsar-admin topics command.

```
./bin/pulsar-admin topics compact  persistent://public/default/
instrument-price
```

Pulsar allows Compacting this topic would give consumers on the topic two options.

- They can read from the original, non-compacted topic if they need access to "historical" values, i.e., the entirety of the topic's messages.

- They can read from the compacted topic if they only want to see the most up-to-date messages.

```
void initialize() throws PulsarClientException {

// Truncated for Brevity

dayEndPriceConsumer = client.newConsumer(JSONSchema.
of(InstrumentClosePrice.class))
            .topic("bond-day-end-price","eq-day-end-price")
            .subscriptionName("portfolio-update")
            .readCompacted(true)
            .subscribe();
}
```

In the preceding code, the consumer subscribes to the compacted topic by specifying the *readCompacted* attribute. You can also specify the attribute for Pulsar functions by using the input-specs command line option as follows.

```
./bin/pulsar-admin functions localrun
 --jar priceCalculator/target/PriceCalculator-1.0-SNAPSHOT-jar-with-
dependencies.jar \
 --classname BondPriceCalculator \
 --name bond-calculator  \
 --inputs day-end-price  \
 --schema-type json \
 --output bond-day-end-price \
 --input-specs {readCompacted: true}
```

Circuit Breaker

Microservice must handle failures as the service can go down due to various reasons. The Circuit Breaker pattern can prevent an application from repeatedly trying to execute an operation that's likely to fail. The service can either function with a fallback value or must wait for the fault to be fixed. These failed requests can block resources and cause bottlenecks. The Circuit Breaker pattern can prevent a service from repeatedly trying an operation that is likely to fail (see Figure 5-9). The Circuit Breaker pattern also enables an application to detect whether the fault has been resolved.

To work with the Circuit breaker pattern, you need a lightweight language-specific library. In Java, the circuit breaker was popularized by Netflix Hystrix, which has been deprecated. Instead, you can implement the circuit breaker by using Resilence4J.

In the WizKap app, the notification service invoked the valuation service to determine user valuations for the population of its mail template. The service is invoked over REST, and the resulting mail is sent using an external service like AWS Simple Email Service (SES). In such a case, you can use the Resilence4J circuit breaker to invoke the valuations service over HTTP.

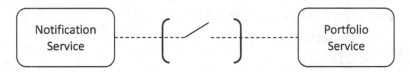

Figure 5-9. *HTTP circuit breaker*

When the valuation service is down, you want to stop consuming messages from subscriptions (see Figure 5-10). The circuit breaker is configured on this layer. Since multiple messages fail when the valuation service is down, the circuit breaker is open (the circuit breaker between consumer service and external service). State transition (CLOSED to OPEN/ HALF_OPEN) of the circuit breaker stops the consumer, so no other messages are processed until the circuit is closed again.

Figure 5-10. *Circuit breaker chaining*

In order to user Resilience4j add resilience4j-circuitbreaker dependency to notification service. You may need to reimport / build the project in your favorite IDE.

```
<dependency>
    <groupId>io.github.resilience4j</groupId>
    <artifactId>resilience4j-circuitbreaker</artifactId>
    <version>1.7.1</version>
</dependency>
```

Next, you need to create a circuit breaker with default values and a custom event consumer that can handle circuit breaker transition events. The transition events provide the required callbacks to pause and resume the subscription. The chapter intends to cover minimum details for Resilence4J , please refer to the documentation of Resilience4j.

```java
void initialize() throws PulsarClientException {
        circuitBreaker = CircuitBreaker.of("http", CircuitBreakerConfig.
        custom()
                    .slidingWindowSize(1).build());
        circuitBreaker.getEventPublisher()
                    .onStateTransition(this::handleEvent);
client = PulsarClient.builder()
                .serviceUrl("pulsar://localhost:6650")
                .build();

// Truncated for Breviity
}

private void handleEvent(CircuitBreakerOnStateTransitionEvent
circuitBreakerOnStateTransitionEvent) {
        if (CircuitBreaker.State.CLOSED.equals(circuitBreakerOnState
        TransitionEvent.getStateTransition().getToState())) {
            notificationConsumer.resume();
        }else{
            notificationConsumer.pause();
        }
    }
}

void readData() throws IOException {
        while (true) {
            Message<UserNotification> msg = notificationConsumer.receive();
            UserNotification notification = msg.getValue();
            Supplier<HttpResponse> supplier = () -> httpClient.
            doRemoteCall();
            HttpResponse httpResponse = circuitBreaker.executeSupplier
            (supplierWithResultHandling);
```

```
        // Truncated for Breviity

    }
}
```

Pulsar allows its consumer to control how they are consuming events options.

- The initialize method creates a circuit breaker with a reference of the handleEvent method for the onStateTransition callback.

- The circuit breaker is invoked in readdata method for fetching data from the portfolio service REST API.

- The handleEvent method checks for the destination state of the transition.

- When the circuit breaker records failure and moves away from the closed state, the notification subscription stops consuming events by invoking the Pause API.

- When the circuit breaker records successful invocations and goes to a closed state, the notification subscription starts consuming events by invoking the resume API.

- Messages that were consumed before paused and not acknowledged are timed out and thus delivered again.

With this approach, your messages stay on queue/topic and are processed again whenever the circuit is closed.

Summary

The chapter discussed Pulsar's out-of-the-box capabilities for building microservice architecture. Integrating APIs, services, data, and systems is one of the most challenging and essential requirements of enterprise software development. Apache Pulsar plays to the strengths of the smart endpoints and dumb pipes principle for enterprise integration. Pulsar clients support integrations of services using the fan-in and fan-out patterns. In a fail fast ecosystem, Pulsar provides support dead-letter queues, retries, and user throttling. Backpressures is supported using backlog quotas and TTL.

Additionally, topic compaction provides a unique capability to record the latest message from a key. All of this is accomplished by taking an example of a portfolio tracker application. In the next chapter, you work with a Pulsar connector to read and write data to external components like databases.

CHAPTER 6

Pulsar Connectors

Pulsar has connectors to simplify connections between the external world, including messaging systems, databases, and other communication channels. Pulsar is connected to a source and a sink.

- **Source**: An external entity that sends data to Pulsar. This can be a file, data pipeline APIs, databases, or so forth. The standard sources in Pulsar are Canal, Debezium MySQL, Debezium PostgreSQL, Debezium MongoDB, DynamoDB, File, Flume, Twitter, Firehose, Kafka, Kinesis, Netty, NSQ, and RabbitMQ.

- **Sink**: An external entity that consumes data from Pulsar. The standard sinks in Pulsar are Aerospike, Cassandra, ElasticSearch, Flume, Hbase, HDFS2, HDFS3, InfluxDB, JDBC ClickHouse, JDBC MariaDB, JDBC PostgreSQL, JDBC SQLite, Kafka, Kinesis, MongoDB, RabbitMQ, Redis, and Solr.

With these connectors, Pulsar provides interfaces and the ability to develop custom connectors. This chapter outlines the IO connectors usage in Apache Pulsar.

Working with Connectors

Using a connector admin CLI or through APIs (REST or SDK), Pulsar connectors can be easily controlled. Connectors (sources and sinks) and functions are components of instances, and they all run on functions workers. An instance of a worker is started when managing a source, sink or function via a connector admin CLI, or a functions admin CLI, or Java SDK.

© Rahul Sharma and Mohammad Atyab 2022
R. Sharma and M. Atyab, *Cloud-Native Microservices with Apache Pulsar*,
https://doi.org/10.1007/978-1-4842-7839-0_6

Depending upon the use case, the source and sink are selected and configured. You first see how few connectors are configured and then build a use case scenario.

Processing Guarantees

The messages that are processed can be set up with processing guarantees. The following are the ones available in Pulsar.

- ATLEAST_ONCE: Every message needs to be sent at least once.

- ATMOST_ONCE: Every message is either sent once only or not set at all.

- EFFECTIVELY_ONCE: Every message is processed only once.

Pulsar manages the guarantees at the source end and makes sure every message follows the selected processing guarantee as Pulsar does the source processing. As opposed to this, sinks control message processing, and therefore the guarantees are respected only when the sink implementation handles the retries as required.

The processing guarantees can be set up when creating or updating the sources or sinks. The sources and sinks are created by pulsar-admin. This can be done using either CLI or Java APIs.

1. Create source/sinks. Set guarantees at this time.

The following example uses a source.

```
$ ./bin/pulsar-admin sources create \
  --processing-guarantees {{PROCESSING-GUARANTEE}}
 ...OTHER CONFIGS
```

The following example uses a source.

```
$ ./bin/pulsar-admin sinks create \
  --processing-guarantees {{PROCESSING-GUARANTEE}}
 ...OTHER CONFIGS
  PROCESSING-GUARANTEE can be one of ATLEAST_ONCE, ATMOST_ONCE or
  EFFECTIVELY_ONCE.
```

The following example uses Java.

```
SourceConfig sourceConfig = SourceConfig.builder()
```

```
            .processingGuarantees(FunctionConfig.ProcessingGuarantees.
            ATLEAST_ONCE)
            .tenant("public")
    //removed for brevity
```

In the preceding code, the source config object has the required processing guarantee. You see how to create a source/sink later in this chapter.

2. Update source/sinks. Set guarantees at this time.

The following example uses a source.

```
$ ./bin/pulsar-admin sources update --processing-guarantees
{{PROCESSING-GUARANTEE}}
  ...OTHER CONFIGS
```

The following example uses a sink.

```
$ ./bin/pulsar-admin sinks update --processing-guarantees {{PROCESSING-
GUARANTEE}}
  ...OTHER CONFIGS
```

PROCESSING-GUARANTEE can be ATLEAST_ONCE, ATMOST_ONCE, or EFFECTIVELY_ONCE.

Using Connectors

pulsar-admin (either CLI or SDK APIs) is required to run a sink or a source. First, let's learn the basic commands to run a source or a sink and see some examples.

Running Sources

The admin command that is needed to be run is of the following format.

```
$ ./bin/pulsar-admin sources create --classname  <classname> --archive
<jar-location> --tenant <tenant> --namespace <namespace> --name <source-
name> --destination-topic-name <output-topic>
```

eg $./bin/pulsar-admin sources create --classname org.apache.pulsar.
io.rabbitmq.RabbitMQSource --archive ~/application.jar --tenant test
--namespace ns1 --name twitter-source --destination-topic-name twitter_data

This command creates a source and submits the topic data to a Pulsar cluster. Instead of submitting a source to run on an existing Pulsar cluster, the source can be run as a process on a local machine.

```
$ ./bin/pulsar-admin sources localrun --classname org.apache.
pulsar.io.rabbitmq.RabbitMQSource --archive connectors/pulsar-io-
rabbitmq-2.8.0.nar --tenant test --namespace ns1 --name twitter-source
--destination-topic-name rabbitmq_data
```

The following are the parameters.

- **class-name**: The name of the class that implements the connector; for example, org.apache.pulsar.io.rabbitmq.RabbitMQSource

- **archive**: The JAR or NAR file contains the path to the compiled classes; for example, pulsar-io-rabbitmq-2.8.0.nar.

  Class name and archive are not required if the source-type is defined.

- **source-type**: Pulsar creates predefined types. The available types can be fetched from Pulsar-admin using the following command.

  The following is a CLI example.

  ```
  $ ./bin/pulsar-admin sources available-sources
  ```

  The following is a Java example.

```
private Set<String> getAllBuiltinSourceTypes(String adminUrl) {
    try {
        return getPulsarAdmin(adminUrl)
                .sources().getBuiltInSources().stream().map
                (ConnectorDefinition::getName).collect(Collectors.toSet());
    } catch (PulsarAdminException e) {
    }
    return new HashSet<>();
}
```

The sources returned from this command can be specified.

- **destination-topic-name:** The topic name this source sends messages on. The consumer(s) need the topic name to receive the messages from the source.

Running Sinks

A sink can be submitted to Pulsar cluster using the following command.

```
$ ./bin/pulsar-admin sinks create --classname  <classname> --archive <jar-
location> --tenant test --namespace <namespace> --name <sink-name> --inputs
<input-topics>
```

An example of running a Cassandra sink in a cluster.

```
$ ./bin/pulsar-admin sinks create --classname org.apache.pulsar.
io.cassandra --archive ~/application.jar --tenant test --namespace ns1
--name cassandra-sink --inputs test_topic
```

To run on local instead of a cluster, use `localrun` instead of `create`.

Monitoring Connectors

Since sources are specialized Pulsar functions, the admin CLI commands can monitor them. The commands are available in admin CLI and Java SDK.

1. Get the connector metadata.

```
$ bin/pulsar-admin functions get \
    --tenant <tenant> \
    --namespace <namespace> \
    --name <connector-name>
public SourceConfig getSource (String adminUrl, String sourceName)
throws IOException {
    try {
        return getPulsarAdmin(adminUrl).sources().getSource("public",
        "default", sourceName);
    } catch (PulsarAdminException e) {
```

```
            e.printStackTrace();
        }
        return null;
    }
```

2. Get the connector running status.

The following is a CLI example.

```
$bin/pulsar-admin functions getstatus \
    --tenant <tenant> \
    --namespace <namespace> \
    --name <connector-name>
```

The following is a Java example.

```
public SourceStatus getSourceStatus (String adminUrl, String sourceName)
throws IOException {
    try {
        return getPulsarAdmin(adminUrl).sources().
        getSourceStatus("public", "default", sourceName);
    } catch (PulsarAdminException e) {
        e.printStackTrace();
    }
    return null;
}
```

Sample Source Connectors

To connect the sources, the configuration file is required to be set up first. The configuration can be in JSON or YAML format. Every connector has a separate connection file. You see now how to create and connect the following sources in detail: File Source and MySQL.

File Source Connector

Set up configuration using a JSON/YAML file. For the sake of brevity, let's look at the YAML file.

1. Save the following in a file named file-config.yaml.

```
configs:
    inputDirectory: "/home/user/inputDirectory"
    recurse: true
    keepFile: true
    fileFilter: "[^\\.].*"
    pathFilter: "*"
    minimumFileAge: 0
    maximumFileAge: 9999999999
    minimumSize: 1
    maximumSize: 5000000
    ignoreHiddenFiles: true
    pollingInterval: 5000
    numWorkers: 1
```

Description of the config keys:

- **inputDirectory**: The directory to pull the changes from. This is the only mandatory configuration.

- **fileFilter**: If recurring is true, use this regex to filter the files.

- **recurse**: recursively read the data from subdirectories. The default is true.

- **pathFilter**: If recurring is true, use this regex to filter the files. The default is null.

- **keepFile**: After reading the file, is it required to be kept or de deleting. The default is false.

- **minimumFileAge**: Any file that is having age less than this config is ignored. The default is 0.

- **mimumFileAge**: The maximum age of the file to be processed. The default is Long.MAX_VALUE.

- **minimumSize**: The minimum size (in bytes) of the file to be processed. The default is 1.

- **maximumSize**: The maximum size (in bytes) of the file to be processed. The default is Double.MAX_VALUE.

- **ignoreHiddenFiles**: Processing of hidden files is required or not. By default, this is 0.

- **pollingInterval**: A polling interval (long) defines the time interval, after which directory tracking needs to be done (in ms). The default value is 10000.

- **numWorkers**: For large files, multiple threads can read the file(s). By default, it is 1.

2. Download MySQL connector pulsar-io-file-2.8.0.nar from `http://pulsar.apache.org/en/download/` and place it in a new folder named connectors. This file is used as the archive in the next step.

3. Create a source using pulsar-admin. Admin APIs can be called either through code or using CLI commands.

Using Java code:

```
public boolean createSource (String adminUrl) {
    SourceConfig sourceConfig = SourceConfig.builder()
            .processingGuarantees(FunctionConfig.ProcessingGuarantees.
            ATLEAST_ONCE)
            .tenant("public")
            .namespace("default")
            .topicName("test-file-topic")
            .name("test-file-source")
            .archive("connectors/pulsar-io-file-2.8.0.nar")
            .schemaType("yaml")
            .build();
```

```
try {
    getPulsarAdmin(adminUrl).sources().createSource(sourceConfig,
    "file-config.yaml");
getPulsarAdmin(adminUrl).sources().startSource("public", "default",
"test-file-source");
    return true;
} catch (PulsarAdminException e) {
    e.printStackTrace();
}
return false;
}
```

SourceConfig object is required to be created first using SourceConfigBuilder and set required parameters like tenant name, namespace, topic name to be created, source name, and archive name.

First, the createSource API needs to be called, and then the startSource API is called. The following is a CLI example.

```
$ bin/pulsar-admin sources localrun \
--archive connectors/pulsar-io-file-2.8.0.nar \
--name test-file-source \
--destination-topic-name test-file-topic \
--source-config-file file-config.yaml
```

The tenant and namespace parameters are self-explanatory. A topic name on which the data can be consumed is required. A source name also needs to be mentioned when creating the source. Source-config-file flag contains the name of the file in which configuration was saved in the last step.

Additionally, you can set the – processing-guarantees flag to set the guarantees.

At this point, a topic is started, and the following logs can be seen.

```
INFO  org.apache.pulsar.client.impl.ProducerImpl - [pulsar-file-
test] [standalone-11-0] Created producer on cnx [id: 0x0e2a674d,
L:/127.0.0.1:55658 - R:localhost/127.0.0.1:6650]
```

4. Start a consumer to read the changes in the file.

```
$ ./bin/pulsar-client consume -s file-test -n 0  test-file-topic
```

5. Write some changes in the directory.

```
$ echo "Adding new message!" >> /home/user/inputDirectory/test.txt
```

The consumer terminal window shows the following message.

```
----- got message -----
Adding new message!
```

6. Clean up. Stop the source created in the preceding steps.

- Using CLI.

```
$ ./bin/pulsar-admin sources stop --name test-file-source --tenant
public -namespace default
```

- Using Java, call to stop the source with tenant name, namespace, and source name to stop the connector source.

```java
public boolean stopSource (String adminUrl, String tenant, String
namespace, String sourceName) {
    try {
        getPulsarAdmin(adminUrl).sources().stopSource(tenant, namespace,
        sourceName);
        return true;
    } catch (PulsarAdminException e) {
        e.printStackTrace();
    }
    return false;
}
```

MySQL Source Connector

Let's look at implementing a MySQL source connector (implemented by Debezium) in the following steps.

1. Start the stand-alone Pulsar service. The steps of starting a stand-alone Pulsar instance have been described in Chapter 1.

2. Start a MySQL server. Run a server with the server that contains a database example, and Debezium captures the changes made. Open a new terminal to start a new container that runs a MySQL database server preconfigured with a database named inventory.

```
$ docker run --rm --name mysql -p 3306:3306 -e MYSQL_ROOT_
PASSWORD=root -e MYSQL_USER=mysqluser -e MYSQL_PASSWORD=mysqlpw
debezium/example-mysql:0.9
```

The command displays the following.

```
2021-09-15T23:39:52.547035Z 0 [Note] Event Scheduler: Loaded 0 events
2021-09-15T23:39:52.547410Z 0 [Note] mysqld: ready for connections.
Version: '5.7.25-log' socket: '/var/run/mysqld/mysqld.sock' port:
3306  MySQL Community Server (GPL)
```

3. Download MySQL connector pulsar-io-debezium-mysql-2.8.0.nar from http://pulsar.apache.org/en/download/. Place it in a new folder named connectors. This file is used as the archive in the next step.

4. Define the configs according to the requirements. The configuration is specific to connectors. The configuration can be either in a JSON file or a YAML file. For MySQL and Postgres, the configurations are as follows.

```
tenant: "test-tenant"
namespace: "mysql-namespace"
name: "debezium-mysql-source"
topicName: "debezium-mysql-topic"
archive: "connectors/pulsar-io-debezium-mysql-2.8.0.nar" #downloaded
class archive in step 3
#The parallelism factor of a Pulsar #Function (i.e. the number of
function instances to run)
parallelism: 1
configs:
#This is the class for connector that implements the connector
#task
```

```
    task.class: "io.debezium.connector.mysql.MySqlConnectorTask"
# config for mysql, docker image: debezium/example-mysql:0.8
 #db host
    database.hostname: "localhost"
#db port
database.port: "3306" #db port
#db user name
    database.user: "debezium"
#db password
    database.password: "dbz"
#A connector id that is unique for this cluster
    database.server.id: "987654"
#This is a logical name of the server or cluster.
    database.server.name: "dbserver1"
#This is the list of database names which will be monitored by
#the connectors
 database.whitelist: "inventory"

#This is the history class of the db
database.history: "org.apache.pulsar.io.debezium.PulsarDatabaseHistory"

#Interal usage topic, not to be used by consumers. The history
#of db is written in this topic. It can be used for recovering
#DDL statements
database.history.pulsar.topic: "history-topic"

#Pulsar service URL for histroy is mentioned either in Pulsar
#protocol or http/https format
database.history.pulsar.service.url: "pulsar://127.0.0.1:6650"

#The class that is provided  by Kafka Connector to convert
#record key
key.converter: "org.apache.kafka.connect.json.JsonConverter"

#The class that is provided  by Kafka Connector to convert
#record value
value.converter: "org.apache.kafka.connect.json.JsonConverter"
#Pulsar service URL for histroy is mentioned either in Pulsar
```

```
#protocol or http/https format
pulsar.service.url: "pulsar://127.0.0.1:6650"

#This topic monitors the last offset successfully completed by
#this connector
offset.storage.topic: "offset-topic"
```

Save the configuration file and name it debezium-mysql-source-config.yaml.

    5.   Run the Pulsar connector with the config file.

```
bin/pulsar-admin source localrun  --sourceConfigFile debezium-mysql-
source-config.yaml
```

On successful running of the source connector, the following messages are seen.

```
22:26:46.958 [pulsar-client-io-1-2] INFO  org.apache.pulsar.client.
impl.ProducerImpl - [persistent://public/default/dbserver1.inventory.
products_on_hand] [null] Creating producer on cnx [id: 0xf3269fce,
L:/127.0.0.1:56372 - R:localhost/127.0.0.1:6650]
22:26:46.995 [pulsar-client-io-1-2] INFO  org.apache.pulsar.client.
impl.ProducerImpl - [persistent://public/default/dbserver1.inventory.
products_on_hand] [standalone-0-8] Created producer on cnx [id: 0xf3269fce,
L:/127.0.0.1:56372 - R:localhost/127.0.0.1:6650]
22:26:47.024 [pulsar-client-io-22-1] INFO  org.apache.pulsar.io.kafka.
connect.AbstractKafkaConnectSource - Finished flushing offsets to storage
22:26:47.024 [pulsar-client-io-22-1] INFO  org.apache.pulsar.client.impl.
ConsumerImpl - [offset-topic][reader-a9cc3b6e5a] Get topic last message Id
22:26:47.026 [pulsar-client-io-22-1] INFO  org.apache.pulsar.client.
impl.ConsumerImpl - [offset-topic][reader-a9cc3b6e5a] Successfully
getLastMessageId 524:1
22:26:47.027 [pulsar-client-internal-24-1] INFO  org.apache.pulsar.client.
impl.ConsumerImpl - [offset-topic][reader-a9cc3b6e5a] Get topic last
message Id
22:26:47.029 [pulsar-client-io-22-1] INFO  org.apache.pulsar.client.
impl.ConsumerImpl - [offset-topic][reader-a9cc3b6e5a] Successfully
getLastMessageId 524:1
22:26:47.074 [blc-localhost:3306] INFO  io.debezium.util.Threads - Creating
thread debezium-mysqlconnector-dbserver1-binlog-client
```

```
....
22:26:47.110 [blc-localhost:3306] INFO  io.debezium.connector.mysql.
BinlogReader - Connected to MySQL binlog at localhost:3306, starting at
binlog file 'mysql-bin.000003', pos=154, skipping 0 events plus 0 rows
...
```

Run the following command to check the list of available topics.

```
$ ./bin/pulsar-admin topics list public/default
"persistent://public/default/dbserver1.inventory.customers"
"persistent://public/default/dbserver1.inventory.products_on_hand"
"persistent://public/default/offset-topic"
"persistent://public/default/dbserver1"
"persistent://public/default/dbserver1.inventory.addresses"
"persistent://public/default/dbserver1.inventory.orders"
"persistent://public/default/dbserver1.inventory.products"
"persistent://public/default/history-topic"
"persistent://public/default/debezium-mysql-topic"
```

There are multiple topics generated by the MySQL connector. Every table has its own topic, as seen in the result, and data can be consumed for these topics. There are internal topics generated to store history and offset. These topics are history-topic and offset-topic.

6. Subscribe to the Pulsar topics to monitor the MySQL changes. The next step is to consume the data produced after the changes are done in the MySQL tables. For example, subscribe to order table changes or send information about new orders to a third party.

    ```
    $ bin/pulsar-client consume -s "new orders" public/default/
    dbserver1.inventory.orders -n 0
    ```

7. Make changes in MySQL Server, and verify that the changes are recorded in Pulsar topics.

Run the following command to access the MySQL shell.

```
$ docker run -it --rm --name mysqlterm --link mysql --rm mysql:5.7
sh -c 'exec mysql -h"$MYSQL_PORT_3306_TCP_ADDR" -P"$MYSQL_
PORT_3306_TCP_PORT" -uroot -p"$MYSQL_ENV_MYSQL_ROOT_PASSWORD"'
```

The SQL shell opens, and further changes can be done in the tables. You add a new order row and check how the consumer receives the newly inserted rows.

```
mysql> use inventory;
mysql> show tables;
+----------------------+
| Tables_in_inventory  |
+----------------------+
| addresses            |
| customers            |
| orders               |
| products             |
| products_on_hand     |
+----------------------+
mysql> select * from orders;
+--------------+------------+-----------+----------+------------+
| order_number | order_date | purchaser | quantity | product_id |
+--------------+------------+-----------+----------+------------+
|        10001 | 2016-01-16 |      1001 |        1 |        102 |
|        10002 | 2016-01-17 |      1002 |        2 |        105 |
|        10003 | 2016-02-19 |      1002 |        2 |        106 |
|        10004 | 2016-02-21 |      1003 |        1 |        107 |
+--------------+------------+-----------+----------+------------+
mysql> insert into inventory.orders (order_number, order_date, purchaser,
quantity, product_id) values (2001, CURDATE(), 1002, 2, 105);

Query OK, 1 row affected (0.01 sec)
```

Next, an order insertion message is received by the consumer created in step 6.

```
----- got message -----
key:[eyJvcmRlcl9udW1iZXIiOjIwMDF9], properties:[], content:{"before":null,"
after":{"order_number":2001,"order_date":18891,"purchaser":1002,"quantity":
2,"product_id":105},"source":{"version":"1.0.0.Final","connector":"mysql","
```

name":"dbserver1","ts_ms":1632209172000,"snapshot":"false","db":"inventory"
,"table":"orders","server_id":223344,"gtid":null,"file":"mysql-bin.000003",
"pos":362,"row":0,"thread":5,"query":null},"op":"c","ts_ms":1632209172292}
```
12:56:38.941 [pulsar-timer-5-1] INFO  org.apache.pulsar.client.impl.
ConsumerStatsRecorderImpl - [public/default/dbserver1.inventory.orders]
[sub-products] [15616] Prefetched messages: 0 --- Consume throughput
received: 0.02 msgs/s --- 0.00 Mbit/s --- Ack sent rate: 0.02 ack/s ---
Failed messages: 0 --- batch messages: 0 ---Failed acks: 0
```

8. Clean up. When required, you need to kill all the processes you
created and Pulsar if required.

   a. Close MySql. First, quit the MySQL shell if it is open, using the quit
   command.

   ```
   mysql> quit
   ```

   b. Close Docker, either through the Docker dashboard or kill the process using
   the commands.

   ```
   $ docker ps
   CONTAINER ID    IMAGE…
   2a415d0a921a    debezium/example-mysql:0.9...
   $docker kill 2a415d0a921a
   ```

   c. Stop the standalone Pulsar using the Ctrl + C command.

   d. To delete Pulsar data, go to the Pulsar directory.

   ```
   $rm -fr data
   ```

Sink Connectors

The configuration file must first be set up to connect the sources. The configuration can
be in JSON or YAML format. Every connector has a separate connection file. You see now
how to create and connect the following sources in detail: File Source and MySQL.

Sample Sink Connector

Similar to sources, to connect the sinks, the configuration file must first be set up. The configuration can be in JSON or YAML format. Every connector has a separate connection file. You see now how to create and connect the following sources in detail: Redis and Twitter.

Table 6-1 describes the Redis configurations.

Table 6-1. *Redis Configurations*

Name	Type	Default	Required	Description
redisHosts	String	" " (empty string)	true	Comma separated list of Redis hosts
redisPassword	String	" " (empty string)	false	The password to connect to Redis
redisDatabase	int	0	true	The Redis database to connect to
clientMode	String	Standalone	false	The client mode when interacting with Redis cluster: standalone or cluster
autoReconnect	boolean	true	false	Automatically reconnect to the Redis client
requestQueue	int	Integer.MAX_VALUE ie 2147483647	false	The maximum number of queued requests to Redis
tcpNoDelay	boolean	false	false	Enable TCP with no delay
keepAlive	boolean	false	false	Enable a keepalive to Redis
connectTimeout	long	10000	false	Wait time before marking as time out when connecting (in ms)
operationTimeout	long	10000	false	Wait time before marking as time out for operations (in ms)
batchTimeMs	int	1000	false	The Redis batch operation time in (ms)
batchSize	int	200	false	The batch size of writing to Redis db

The following are the steps to start a Pulsar sink.

1. The configs are put into a JSON or a YAML file. For the sake of
    brevity, let's look at a JSON file.

```
{
    "redisHosts": "localhost:6379",
    "redisPassword": "password@1234",
    "redisDatabase": "1",
    "clientMode": "Standalone",
    "operationTimeout": "2000",
    "batchSize": "100",
    "batchTimeMs": "1000",
    "connectTimeout": "3000"
}
```

Save this file into a JSON file named pulsar-redis-sink.json.

2. Create a sink using the pulsar-admin CLI.

```
bin/pulsar-admin sinks create \
--archive connectors/pulsar-io-redis-2.8.0.nar
--inputs pulsar-redis-sink-topic \
--name pulsar-postgres-jdbc-sink \
--sink-config-file connectors/pulsar-postgres-jdbc-sink.yaml \
--parallelism 1
```

- archive: The sink needs the archive and YAML file to be configured.

- pulsar-redis-sink-topic: As you know that a Pulsar sink
  subscribes to a topic, you need to specify the topic the sink listens to.

Developing IO Connectors

Pulsar IO connectors can be created by implementing the required interfaces.

- To create a connector that reads data from a data source, the org.
  apache.pulsar.io.core.Source interface must be implemented.

- To create a connector that read data from a data source, the `org.apache.pulsar.io.core.Sink` interface must be implemented.

- To create a connector that reads and writes to Pulsar, both interfaces must be implemented.

The last step is to package them into a JAR or a NAR file.

Developing a Source IO Connector

The `org.apache.pulsar.io.core.Source` interface needs three methods to be implemented.

- **open()**

  - Takes two parameters.

  - Map<String, Object> config holds the parameters required for the configuration of the connector. These configurations are passed in a YAML or JSON file, which is made available to the connector using this parameter.

  - SourceContext gets metadata like output topic name, source name, parallelism, and processing guarantees.

  - This method is used for opening connections to the data source and ready it for reading data.

- **read()**

  - In this method, the logic of reading from the data source is implemented. The return type is `org.apache.pulsar.functions.api.Record<T>`.

  - If record read is successful, `org.apache.pulsar.functions.api.Record#ack()` is sent and `org.apache.pulsar.functions.api.Record#fail()`, if failed to set the record.

- **close()**

  - Each source extends `java.lang.AutoCloseable` interface. Hence, implementing this method is an essential best practice to close all the connections to the data source and free up resources.

For NAR packaging, refer to the pom.xml for nifi-nar-maven-plugin.

```
<plugins>
  <plugin>
    <groupId>org.apache.nifi</groupId>
    <artifactId>nifi-nar-maven-plugin</artifactId>
    <version>1.2.0</version>
  </plugin>
</plugins>
```

Developing a Sink IO Connector

The org.apache.pulsar.io.core.Sink interface requires three methods to be implemented.

- **open()**

  - Map<String, Object> config holds the parameters required for the configuration of the connector. These configurations are passed in a YAML or JSON file, which is made available to the connector using this parameter.

  - SinkContext gets metadata like output topic name, source name to be created, parallelism, processing guarantees.

  - This method is used for opening connections to the data sink and ready it for writing data.

  - This method is the right place to open connections to the data source and ready it for writing.

- **write()**

  - In this method, the logic of reading from the data source is implemented. The input type is org.apache.pulsar.functions.api.Record<T>.

  - If record read is successful, org.apache.pulsar.functions.api.Record#ack() is set in the Record object and org.apache.pulsar.functions.api.Record#fail(), if failed to set in the record object.

- Takes one parameter of type `org.apache.pulsar.functions.api.Record<T>`. This method should implement the logic of writing to the data source.

- **close()**

  - Each sink extends `java.lang.AutoCloseable` interface. Hence, implementing this method is an essential best practice to close all the connections to the data source and release it.

For NAR packaging, refer to the pom.xml for nifi-nar-maven-plugin.

```
<plugins>
  <plugin>
    <groupId>org.apache.nifi</groupId>
    <artifactId>nifi-nar-maven-plugin</artifactId>
    <version>1.2.0</version>
  </plugin>
</plugins>
```

Summary

Pulsar IO **connectors** enable developers to easily create, deploy, and manage Pulsar **application**s that interact with external systems. This makes the application more powerful since the Pulsar messaging system can easily be used in conjunction with external systems like databases, cloud services, social media platforms, or any third-party library, making the entire universe available to the application.

CHAPTER 7

Pulsar Security

The previous chapters worked with Apache Pulsar using the HTTP admin API and Pulsar protocol. You deployed functions, created producers, and created sinks and subscribers using these connections. But until now, you have been working purely with plain unencrypted traffic: HTTP or TCP. However, you often need to securely expose endpoints over the Internet for any production usage over TLS. This chapter looks at the capabilities Pulsar provides for encrypting and decrypting network traffic. It extends to client authentication and authorization use cases.

Quick Overview of TLS

TLS encryption is frequently used to protect network traffic against man-in-the-middle attacks and other types of network snooping. Communication takes place over a TLS encrypted channel instead of a cleartext channel. The primary purpose of such security is to protect sensitive data, including usernames and passwords, to authenticate access. Any secret/user-sensitive data should never be transmitted over a plain cleartext connection since it can be intercepted easily by network sniffing software. Using TLS, you can ensure that your data is securely delivered over the Internet, avoiding possible eavesdropping or content alteration.

Traffic over TLS is encrypted when it leaves the source and decrypted at the destination. This decryption is sometimes called TLS termination. This encryption and decryption are typically carried out far below the application layer (in OSI or TCP/IP terms). In general, application-layer code does not need to understand the finer details of TLS, other than specifying configurations. Typically, most programming languages and platforms offer libraries that have been battle-tested and implemented by experts in cryptography.

© Rahul Sharma and Mohammad Atyab 2022
R. Sharma and M. Atyab, *Cloud-Native Microservices with Apache Pulsar*,
https://doi.org/10.1007/978-1-4842-7839-0_7

Note   Although this chapter covers many aspects of working with TLS in Pulsar, an in-depth discussion of TLS is not within the scope of this book. We walk through the practical aspects of working with TLS, which involve acquiring valid TLS certificates from a certificate authority and using them in your client-server configurations.

When connecting to a server with TLS enabled, clients can verify the server's authenticity. This is done by verifying the server's TLS certificate with the certificate authority (CA), which is signed and issued. Clients and servers use this certificate to establish encrypted channels between them. In this way, man-in-the-middle attacks and other attacks can be prevented. Typically, a CA is a trusted third-party, public body, and most browsers are set up automatically. A private CA may issue certificates for internal intranet sites on large private enterprise networks, and this private CA is automatically trusted on enterprise-managed devices.

Generally, TLS encrypts HTTP traffic on the web, but it is used to encrypt plain TCP traffic in this chapter. In doing so, you work with the different capabilities offered by Apache Pulsar.

TLS Termination

Conventionally, the Pulsar operates on 6650 and 8080 ports for data exchange and admin commands, respectively. TLS communication recommends using an alternative port, even though you can enable those ports for TLS data exchanges. Pulser documentation recommends using 8433 and 6651 for enabling TLS. You would need to change the Pulsar broker to enable listening on these ports. But before you can accomplish this, you need to have TLS certificates that are used for encryption.

Prerequisites

In production and Internet-facing systems, TLS certificates are often issued by a certificate authority. But for consumption internal to an enterprise/team, you should rely on centrally generated signed certificates. If you intend to use the internal certificate authority for more than just testing purposes, make sure to establish proper security measurements. As a prerequisite, generate a set of self-signed certificates using the steps outlined next.

First, you need to have a CA certificate. The certificate is used for various purposes, such as issuing certificates for the Pulsar server and validation in Pulsar clients. You would need a private key for the CA. Create the key using the following command.

```
$ openssl genrsa 2048 > ca-key.pem
```

Next, using this private key, generate an X509 certificate for the CA with the following command. The command allows you to specify a validity period, provided as 10000 days for the certificate.

```
$ openssl req -new -x509 -nodes -days 10000 \
    -key ca-key.pem \
    -out ca-cert.pem
```

Tip   Please make a note of providing valid values, and not blanks, for the asked prompts.

Now that you have the CA certificate, you can begin generating the public and private keys for the Pulsar server (see Figure 7-1). The keys create a certificate signing request (CSR). The CSR file contains the public key and other information that must be included in the certificate (such as the domain name, organization, email address, etc.). CSR and key pair generation are normally performed on the server where the certificate is installed. A CSR can contain various information depending on the validity level and intended use of the certificate. While the public key is shared with the CA (and other parties), the server's private key is kept private and shouldn't be revealed to anyone.

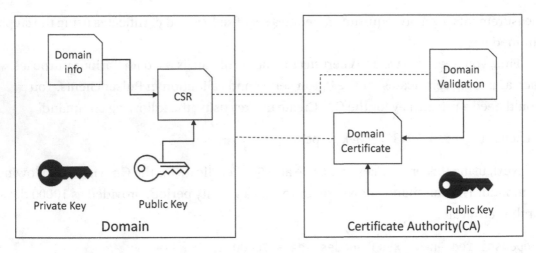

Figure 7-1. *Certificate generation*

Create a server key along with the request using the following command.

```
$ openssl req -newkey rsa:2048 -nodes -days 365000 -keyout server-key.pem
-out server-req.pem
```

Tip   Please make a note of providing valid values, and not blanks, for the prompts.

Generate an X509 certificate for the server using the CSR and the CA certificates generated earlier.

```
$ openssl x509 -req -days 365000 -set_serial 01 \
   -in server-req.pem \
   -out server-cert.pem \
   -CA ca-cert.pem \
   -CAkey ca-key.pem
```

The preceding command generates server-cert.pem, which is specified in the Pulsar configuration. The server presents the certificate to all clients who need to verify the certificate's integrity before proceeding.

Next, let's verify the certificate using the following command.

```
$ openssl verify -CAfile ca-cert.pem ca-cert.pem server-cert.pem
ca-cert.pem: OK
server-cert.pem: OK
```

Configuring the Broker

The first step in TLS is enabling the new TLS ports for both the Pulsar protocol and admin APIs. While doing so, please make a note of disabling the non-TLS ports. Since the broker is responsible for all communication, the necessary changes must be done in broker.conf.

```
# brokerServicePort=6650
brokerServicePortTls=6651
# Port to use to server HTTP request
# webServicePort=8080
webServicePortTls=8443
```

Once the ports are enabled, you must specify the TLS specific parameters. The following options configure the TLS protocol exchange along with the server certificates and the private key. The changes are again part of broker.conf.

```
# Path for the TLS certificate file
tlsCertificateFilePath=/my-ca/server-cert.pem
# Path for the TLS private key file
tlsKeyFilePath= /my-ca/server-key.pem
tlsProtocols=TLSv1.3,TLSv1.2,TLSv1
tlsCiphers=TLS_RSA_WITH_AES_256_CBC_SHA,TLS_RSA_WITH_AES_128_CBC_SHA
```

It is important to note the TLS protocol version and supported TLS ciphers. The Java Runtime provides this for Apache Pulsar. These options work well with JDK 8. Now you can start Pulsar brokers.

Configuring the Client

Now that the server is running on TLS ports, you must configure the client to connect to TLS ports. Additionally, the client must verify the certificate presented by the server on a handshake. This is accomplished by using the ca-cert file certificate verification. If you are using the command line tools, the following options must be specified in the client. conf file.

```
# For TLS:
webServiceUrl=https://localhost:8443/
# webServiceUrl=http://localhost:8080/
```

```
# For TLS:
brokerServiceUrl=pulsar+ssl://localhost:6651/
# brokerServiceUrl=pulsar://localhost:6650/
```

```
tlsTrustCertsFilePath=/my-ca/ca-cert.pem
tlsEnableHostnameVerification=false
```

TLS encryption also supports Server Name Indication (SNI), which allows a client to verify the server's domain name performing the handshake. This is an additional benefit that can be turned off for local/internal systems. Configure the tlsEnableHostnameVerification parameter to toggle off the check. After saving the configuration, you can use the client and the admin API, which should work as expected.

```
$ bin/pulsar-client produce plaintext --messages "AttackAtOnce"
```

```
$ bin/pulsar-client consume encrypt-data -s "cipher-subscription" -n 0
```

```
$ ./bin/pulsar-admin tenants list
```

Pulsar Client also provides API to configure TLS for producers and subscribers. All required options are provided before creating the connection.

```
PulsarClient client = PulsarClient.builder()
                .serviceUrl("pulsar+ssl://localhost:6651/")
                .tlsTrustCertsFilePath("/my-ca/ca-cert.pem")
                .enableTlsHostnameVerification(false)
                .allowTlsInsecureConnection(false)
                .build();
```

Mutual TLS

So far, you have secured the information exchange from client to server. But a typical pulsar client has a two-way connection. Producers send data to the server while consumers receive data from the server. Thus, Pulsar supports mutual TLS (mTLS), which requires the server and its clients to exchange their certificates. This ensures that the parties at each end of a network connection are who they claim to be by verifying that they both have the correct private key (see Figure 7-2). mTLS helps ensure that traffic is secure and trusted in both directions between a client and server.

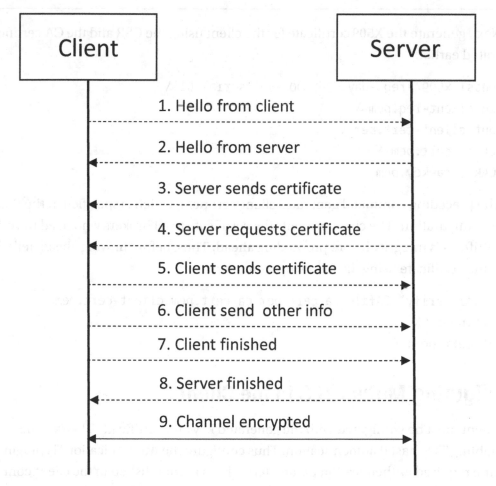

Figure 7-2. *Mutual TLS*

To work with mTLS, the client must have its own set of keys and certificates. You can generate them in the same manner as you did for the server, key, and certificate using the following commands.

```
$ openssl req -newkey rsa:2048 -nodes -days 365000 -keyout client-key.pem
-out client-req.pem
```

Tip   Please make a note of providing valid values, and not blanks, for the asked prompts.

Next, generate the X509 certificate for the client using the CSR and the CA certificates generated earlier.

```
$ openssl x509 -req -days 365000 -set_serial 01 \
    -in client-req.pem \
    -out client-cert.pem \
    -CA ca-cert.pem \
    -CAkey ca-key.pem
```

The preceding command generates client-cert.pem, which is specified in the Pulsar client configuration. The client presents the certificate to all brokers who need to verify the certificate's integrity before proceeding ahead. Thus, before moving ahead, let's first verify the certificate using the following command.

```
$ openssl verify -CAfile ca-cert.pem ca-cert.pem client-cert.pem
ca-cert.pem: OK
client-cert.pem: OK
```

Configuring Mutual TLS in the Client

The client must be configured with the generated key and certificate. This is done by enabling TLS-based authentication. Thus configure the AuthenticationTls plugin with the required authentication parameters. The is accomplished in the client.conf configuration by adding the following parameters.

```
authPlugin=org.apache.pulsar.client.impl.auth.AuthenticationTls
```

```
authParams=tlsCertFile:/my-ca/client-cert.pem,tlsKeyFile:/my-ca/
client-key.pem
```

Pulsar client provides API to provide the required authentication parameters while configuring the connection. You can configure these values for the producers and consumers as follows.

```
client = PulsarClient.builder()
        .serviceUrl("pulsar+ssl://localhost:6651/")
        .tlsTrustCertsFilePath("/my-ca/ca-cert.pem")
        .enableTlsHostnameVerification(false)
        .allowTlsInsecureConnection(false)
        .authentication("org.apache.pulsar.client.impl.auth.Authenticat
        ionTls","tlsCertFile:/my-ca/client-cert.pem,tlsKeyFile:/my-ca/
        client-key.pem ")
        .build();
```

Note   Function workers are enabled using admin API, and thus mTLS configuration must be enabled for function workers. If this is not done, the broker fails when enabling function support. Alternatively, if not required, you can disable function-worker by passing `--no-functions-worker --no-stream-storage` command options.

Configuring Mutual TLS in the Broker

Pulsar broker needs to be enabled for client certificate verification. This configuration is an extension to the TLS configuration added in the previous section. You must enable the TLS authentication provider and provide the ca-cert.pem file for validating the client-presented certificate.

```
authenticationEnabled=true
authenticationProviders=org.apache.pulsar.broker.authentication.
AuthenticationProviderTls
brokerClientTlsEnabled=true
brokerClientTrustCertsFilePath=/my-ca/certs/ca-cert.pem
```

Additionally, you must enable the `tlsRequireTrustedClientCertOnConnect` check. The check makes sure that trusted client certificates are used for connection. It rejects the connection if the client certificate is not trusted.

```
tlsRequireTrustedClientCertOnConnect=true
```

Now you can restart the broker. After the broker, you can reconnect using the console client and using the publisher.

JSON Web Token

JSON Web Token (JWT) is an open standard that defines a compact and self-contained way for securely transmitting information between parties as a JSON object. The token is a JSON-encoded representation of a claim or claims transferred between server and clients (see Figure 7-3). The token is a URL-safe string that can contain an unlimited amount of data. When a server receives a JWT, it can trust its data as the source cryptographically signs the JWT. JWT guards against information tampering as it can't be modified.

It's important to note that a JWT guarantees data ownership but not encryption. Anyone can intercept the token to see the JSON data you stored into a JWT as it's only serialized and not encrypted. For this reason, it is highly recommended to use TLS with JWT.

Authorization is one of the most common JWT use cases. A client can initiate a handshake and generate a valid JWT. The server can then validate the JWT. Afterward, each used call can include the JWT to identify the user and its roles.

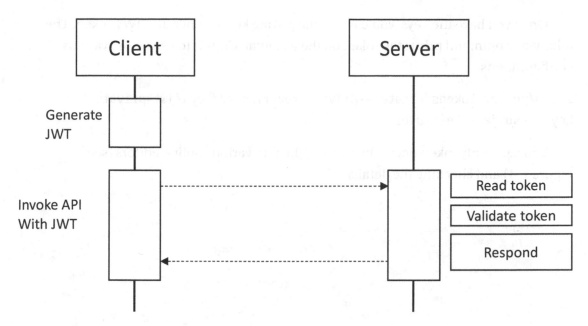

Figure 7-3. *JWT exchange*

Pulsar also allows you to use JWT for mTLS authentication (and authorization). The JWT token is used for client authentication, whereas the broker is authenticated using TLS.

Creating a Token

First, you need a pair of public-private keys for working with JWT. You can use the private client key generate in PEM format for encoding data. But the JWT specification recommends using an algorithm from a list of 12 standards for generating JWT signature keys. You can generate a key pair using the default RSA256 with the following command.

```
$ bin/pulsar tokens create-key-pair --output-private-key ~/keys/jwt-
private.key --output-public-key ~/keys/jwt-public.key
```

Tip   Learn more about the JWT signatures at `https://github.com/jwtk/`
`jjwt#signature-algorithms-keys`.

Once you have the keys, you can use the private key to generate a JWT token. The following command prints the token on the terminal. Copy it to use across various configurations.

```
$ bin/pulsar tokens create --private-key file:///keys/jwt-private.
key  --subject test-user
```

You can verify token details by copying them to various online editors (see Figure 7-4) and checking the details.

Figure 7-4. *JWT token details*

Configuring JWT in the Client

Next, you must configure the client to present the JWT token. The previous section used the TLS certificate by using an appropriate authentication plugin on a similar line to enable AuthenticationToken and configure it with the required parameters.

```
authPlugin=org.apache.pulsar.client.impl.auth.AuthenticationToken
authParams=token:eyJhbGciOiJSUzI1NiJ9.eyJzdWIiOiJoZXN0LXVzZXIifQ.SlLgV_
DLPR2e4zaXRYsV9n4fwWBut-ZfZJ2zM7cuUyXqvY-oHrwU9aT_tKN8Www5VOLu8vkrGgo86HnsK
```

PShdnPdhHpOCLgbcKPWjd1-edu2crZqjKQT9Is9fwu7imlU2YGaXOKTGLNSjafNfUYq77PvaWqS
AMLpXDzwBArNN3GRZNRQTvhzhToBYW37Iv1CK8aP--NQoQmaf8oljcvz6Pg4cNZdaPUeF5afaoq
uQNJDGC7vNGD-CFQBEjY44bTCoi21UwWWI8H5_s6OURXyVkxy_2PhK1C7qGFQAUvbJOv2uzQ2bP
Kmso_Z4wSj7o4s2GEjyf_cOCxx-t4FocprtA

Pulsar SDK clients can configure appropriate APIs to enable JWT authentication with the broker. The API provides many ways to provide the token. Previously, you used the map API in TLS. Alternatively, there is AuthenticationFactory, which can create the details as follows.

```
client = PulsarClient.builder()
    .serviceUrl("pulsar+ssl://localhost:6651")
    .tlsTrustCertsFilePath("/my-ca/ca-cert.pem")
    .enableTlsHostnameVerification(false)
    .allowTlsInsecureConnection(false) .authentication(Authenti
cationFactory.token("eyJhbGciOiJIUzI1NiJ9.eyJzdWIiOiJKb2UifQ.
ipevRNuRP6HflG8cFKnmUPtypruRC4fb1DWtoLL62SY")).build()
```

Configuring JWT in the Broker

The Pulsar broker needs to be enabled for JWT client verification. This configuration is an extension to the TLS configuration added in the previous section. You must enable the TLS authentication provider and provide the public.key file for validating the client-presented credentials.

```
authenticationProviders=org.apache.pulsar.broker.authentication.
AuthenticationProviderToken
brokerClientAuthenticationPlugin=org.apache.pulsar.client.impl.auth.
AuthenticationToken
brokerClientAuthenticationParameters={"token": "eyJhbGciOiJIUzI1NiJ9.
eyJzdWIiOiJoZXN0LXVzZXIifQ.fS3ADOrJNHwxdmnNeyW--N6bgz_6PT6WtnbljbQRjKM"}
tokenSecretKey=file:///keys/jwt-public.key
```

Tip   Please not distribute the JWT-generated public key among all Pulsar brokers.

Now you can restart the broker. Afterward, you can reconnect using the console client and the publisher.

Authorization

Until now, you have worked with authentication, the process of validating that the users are who they claim to be. The next step is authorization, which gives a user permission to access a specific resource or function.

In Pulsar, you can control producer and consumer access at the namespace level. These permissions are associated with roles identified by the authentication process. In the JWT section, you associated user roles with the token by specifying the subject parameter. On the other hand, the TLS authentication uses the common name for role mapping.

Role Grants

In Apache Pulsar, privileges are granted to roles, and roles are associated with users' identities to specify the operations that the users can perform on the various topics in the cluster. It is important to note the by default o grants are applied. Administrators should provide the required grants and setup users before enabling the authorization

You can use the pulsar-admin command line to manage grants. The following are some of the role grants available within Pulsar.

- **Produce** grants a tenant permission to produce messages in a namespace.

- **Consumer** grants a tenant permission to subscribe messages in a namespace.

- **Admin** grants a tenant permission to modify or update attributes.

You can grant namespace permissions, as shown in the following command. The command provides produce and consume permission to any role, such as test.auth, service1.auth, and so forth. These are common names specified in TLS certificates.

```
$./bin/pulsar-admin namespaces grant-permission public/default   --actions
produce,consume   --role *.auth
```

You can also verify these permissions using the following command.

```
$./bin/pulsar-admin namespaces permissions public/default
"*.auth    [produce, consume]"
```

Tenant-level grants are provided while creating tenants or updating the tenets' details using the following command.

```
$./bin/pulsar-admin tenants update public  -r *.auth
```

Tip Please make a note of the role name. You have used regular expressions to allow subdomain CNames. But these can be absolute names that are provided using TLS CNames or JWT subject names.

Configuring Broker for Authorization

Like authentication, authorization must be enabled in the Pulsar broker. Since it uses authentication as the foundation, the configuration is straightforward.

```
authorizationEnabled=true
```

The flag enables validation of grants that were configured in the previous sections. By default, Pulsar does a text lookup; so, using wildcards in the grant expressions does not work. You must enable another configuration that allows Pulsar to perform wildcard-based matching.

```
authorizationAllowWildcardsMatching=true
```

Finally, teams need roles that can allow them to manage the entire Pulsar cluster. Pulsar provides super-user role mappings for this purpose. You can provide additional roles that can be used for Pulsar management.

```
superUserRoles=admin,admin.auth
```

Restart the broker with these changes to make authorization effective immediately.

Configuring the Client for Authorization

The client needs no change. It must perform the handshake using the same TLS authentication as shown next. The API works if configured correctly; otherwise, it fails with `AuthorizationException`.

```
client = PulsarClient.builder()
    .serviceUrl("pulsar+ssl://localhost:6651")
    .tlsTrustCertsFilePath("/my-ca/ca-cert.pem")
    .enableTlsHostnameVerification(false)
    .allowTlsInsecureConnection(false) .authentication(Authentication
    Factory.token("eyJhbGciOiJIUzI1NiJ9.eyJzdWIiOiJKb2UifQ.
    ipevRNuRP6HflG8cFKnmUPtypruRC4fb1DWtoLL62SY")).build()
```

The CLI also works because no configuration parameters were changed. But the admin commands fail since the user is not authorized for tenant management.

```
$ ./bin/pulsar-admin namespaces list public
Unauthorized to validateTenantOperation for originalPrincipal [null]
and clientAppId [test.auth] about operation [LIST_NAMESPACES] on tenant
[public]
```

Summary

This chapter took a quick, surface-level dip into the deep domain of setting up TLS certificates to protect your network traffic. We appreciate that some of you may feel a bit overwhelmed by all the concepts we had to rush through. We have barely scratched the surface of the ecosystem of TLS certificates. However, we feel we have shown the possibilities with Apache Pulsar. You learned to establish a mutual TLS for zero-trust architectures. You extended authentication to authorizations and looked at the fine level of grants available with Apache Pulsar. The next chapter establishes Pulsar in cloud-native environments using various Kubernetes ecosystems.

Deploying Pulsar on Kubernetes

This final chapter explores Apache Pulsar's native integration with the Kubernetes container orchestration platform. Kubernetes is undoubtedly the most popular container microservices platform nowadays. Apache Pulsar integrates tightly with Kubernetes and can act as a first-class citizen in the Kubernetes ecosystem. Previously, you created Pulsar publishers, subscribers, and functions. This chapter explores how to deploy these components in Kubernetes clusters using Pulsar proxy. You also work with Pulsar storage to support high-volume message interexchange.

Note Our focus remains on how Pulsar integrates with the Kubernetes ecosystem rather than the advanced details of Kubernetes itself. You assume that you have a basic familiarity with Kubernetes primitives and restrict our explanations to how Pulsar integrates them.

Setup

The rest of this chapter runs a local Kubernetes cluster on a laptop for Pulsar installation and configuration. Installation of local Kubernetes is beyond the scope of this book, but it should not be too complicated to set up by visiting the official website. You can use either of the following versions, which is best suited to your experience.

- K3s (https://k3s.io/), deployed using k3d
- MicroK8s (https://microk8s.io/), running over multipass on macOS

171

© Rahul Sharma and Mohammad Atyab 2022
R. Sharma and M. Atyab, *Cloud-Native Microservices with Apache Pulsar*,
https://doi.org/10.1007/978-1-4842-7839-0_8

- minikube (https://minikube.sigs.k8s.io/docs/)

These solutions make the setup of some advanced Kubernetes applications very trivial. minikube has been the de facto standard for running the local version of Kubernetes. You may prefer to use any other Kubernetes flavor they like, such as Docker Desktop with Kubernetes enabled.

You can also use a cloud-managed Kubernetes offering. And in fact, you shift to a managed cloud offering in later scenarios. You expect there to be no change needed for Pulsar configuration and installation between local and cloud Kubernetes. The reason for using a cloud offering is again for working with volumes for persistence. You provision a cloud Kubernetes cluster on the Amazon Elastic Kubernetes Service (EKS). You may prefer to use GKE, AKS, or DO if you desire. Most of the steps you outline should work as-is on any Kubernetes distribution.

You already have a local Kubernetes cluster running. All requests to the Kubernetes API server happen through the kubectl CLI, which is typically installed along with local Kubernetes distros. kubectl needs a kube context configuration to point to the target Kubernetes cluster. A typical installation on the Kubernetes cluster consists of the following three components.

- Kubernetes RBAC configuration to give Pulsar sufficient permissions to talk to the API server

- Pulsar binary consisting of brokers, bookies, ZooKeeper, and so on

- Pulsar configuration to cater to various use cases

Prerequisites

You need to generate roles for various components, including broker, admin, and proxy. These are required to secure the communication between the broker, the broker-admin, and the proxy. These credentials are generated as Kubernetes secrets within the namespace where Pulsar components are deployed.

The Pulsar community has provided prepare_helm_release.sh script from the Helm chart repository (https://github.com/apache/pulsar-helm-chart). The script creates JWT secret keys and tokens for the following three superusers.

- broker-admin is the role for interbroker communications.

- proxy-admin is the role for proxies to communicate to brokers.

- admin is the role used by the admin tools.

By default, the script generates an asymmetric public/private key pair. But you can configure it to generate a symmetric secret key by specifying --symmetric option in the command.

```
$ ./scripts/pulsar/prepare_helm_release.sh -n eventing -k pulsar-dev -c
```

Configure Helm

You can install Pulsar on Kubernetes by creating the required configuration by hand. There are several manual steps involved which makes the complete process error-prone. Alternatively, it is recommended to use Helm's package and release manager (`https://helm.sh/`) to install Pulsar on Kubernetes.

In Helm, a deployable artifact is bundled up into a chart that encapsulates all the resources necessary to install and upgrade that software over time, including configuration and dependencies. Pulsar community provides the required Helm chart, which installs/upgrades Pulsar. Helm reuses the current kubeconfig set by kubectl.

Next, the latest Helm v3 is installed and kubeconfig set up to point to the local Kubernetes cluster.

```
$ helm repo add apache https://pulsar.apache.org/charts
"apache" already exists with the same configuration, skipping
```

```
% helm repo update
Hang tight while you grab the latest from your chart repositories...
...Successfully got an update from the "apache" chart repository
Update Complete. ⁕ Happy Helming!⁕
```

Once the chart is added and updated, you can install Pulsar using the latest version of the official Pulsar Helm chart.

Exploring Pulsar Helm Chart

The Pulsar Helm chart installs all components, including bookies, brokers, ZooKeeper, and proxy. Pulsar is exposed to the external world using a Kubernetes service of type *LoadBalancer*. In a Kubernetes *managed* service model, this automatically spins up a cloud load balancer in front of all the Kubernetes nodes and routes all incoming requests to the Pulsar broker. The Helm template also defines some default values, so let's look at some default values from the Helm chart and some other ones you want to customize.

```
## Control what components of Apache Pulsar to deploy for the cluster
components:
  # zookeeper
  zookeeper: true
  # bookkeeper
  bookkeeper: true
  # bookkeeper - autorecovery
  autorecovery: true
  # broker
  broker: true
  # functions
  functions: true
  # proxy
  proxy: true
  # toolset
  toolset: true
  # pulsar manager
  pulsar_manager: true
```

Please note this is not a standard Kubernetes manifest of any kind. These are configuration values in YAML format applied to the actual Kubernetes YAMLs in the Helm chart. The preceding values determine which components are deployed by the Helm chart. By default, it has the following configurations.

- Three instances of Pulsar Brokers run as a Kubernetes statefulset

- Four instances of Pulsar bookies run as a Kubernetes statefulset

- Three instances of Pulsar ZooKeeper run as a Kubernetes statefulset

- Kubernetes runtime for functions

- Exposes pulsar-admin REST API and the Pulser broker binary protocol

- A monitoring stack consisting of Prometheus and Grafana

Brokers are exposed as ClusterIP, making them non-accessible outside the cluster. Instead, there is an instance of Pulsar proxy deployed using the load balancer service.

There are many such entries in the default values.yaml in the Helm chart. We encourage you to explore further configuration on their own. These values can be changed to customize the Pulsar setup for particular use cases. Please note these observations are for the current state of the Helm chart at the time of writing this book. The chart continues to evolve.

Before customizing the values, you can use the `helm template` command to view the default generated deployment manifests. Let's run the command to see what the final configuration looks like. Since there is quite a lot of output, you only focus on a few pieces. You are encouraged to run the command themselves to view the full output.

```
$ helm template pulsar-dev apache/pulsar
```

Since you are deploying on a local cluster, you would like to reduce the instance count of each service. Additionally, if you want to remove a few components, like recovery and monitoring, there are a few tweaks to the default configuration.

```
zookeeper:
  replicaCount: 1
bookkeeper:
  replicaCount: 1
broker:
  replicaCount: 1
  configData:
    # storage settings
    managedLedgerDefaultEnsembleSize: "1"
    managedLedgerDefaultWriteQuorum: "1"
    managedLedgerDefaultAckQuorum: "1"
proxy:
  replicaCount: 1
```

You can validate the configuration by using the `helm template` command with `--values=custom.yaml` option. Let's run the command once again to view the generated deployment manifests with the custom values.

```
$ helm template --values=custom.yml pulsar-dev apache/pulsar
```

Installation

Kubernetes deploys components to a namespace, and it uses the default namespace if unspecified. In production environments, it is often recommended to deploy Pulsar components to only a particular namespace. The. Helm command supports deploying services to various Kubernetes namespaces. Alternatively, the Helm chart supports parameters to deploy and create namespaces.

```
namespace: ""
namespaceCreate: false
```

You stick with the Helm command to deploy to the eventing namespace. Let's now install Pulsar with the Helm command. You then run a few commands to observe it was properly deployed.

```
$ helm install      --values custom.yaml      --set
initialize=true      --namespace eventing  pulsar-dev apache/pulsar
NAME: pulsar-dev
LAST DEPLOYED: Thu Sep 16 20:46:49 2021
NAMESPACE: eventing
STATUS: deployed
REVISION: 1
TEST SUITE: None
```

Pulsar is now installed and running on the cluster. In the context of Kubernetes, there is no difference between installing an application and running it. It is automatically started up within a container. Please note the `--set initialize=true` option since the cluster is bootstrapped, so you must initialize the bookie with Pulsar cluster metadata.

```
$ helm ls -n eventing
NAME            NAMESPACE    REVISION  UPDATED
STATUS          CHART        APP VERSION
pulsar-dev      eventing     1         2021-09-16 20:46:49.930249 +0530 IST
deployed        pulsar-2.7.3    2.7.2
```

Next let's verify the deployed components by looking up executing pods.

```
$ kubectl get pods -n eventing
NAME                                          READY  STATUS     RESTARTS  AGE
pulsar-dev-pulsar-manager-6c6889dff-9m2f8     1/1    Running    0         6h20m
pulsar-dev-bookie-init-jbkgg                  0/1    Completed  0         6h20m
pulsar-dev-pulsar-init-5kggs                  0/1    Completed  0         6h20m
pulsar-dev-zookeeper-0                        1/1    Running    0         6h20m
pulsar-dev-bookie-0                           1/1    Running    0         6h20m
pulsar-dev-broker-0                           1/1    Running    0         6h20m
## Truncated for Brevity
```

If you look up the services, you find out Pulsar has deployed the broker, bookies, and ZooKeeper as ClusterIP. These services are not accessible outside the Kubernetes cluster. But it has also deployed a few more components, like Manager and proxy, as a LoadBalancer service, which makes them accessible externally.

```
$ kubectl get svc -n eventing
NAME                         TYPE         CLUSTER-IP    EXTERNAL-IP
   PORT(S)                                AGE
pulsar-dev-toolset           ClusterIP    None          <none>
   <none>                                 6h21m
pulsar-dev-bookie            ClusterIP    None          <none>
   3181/TCP,8000/TCP                      6h21m
pulsar-dev-prometheus        ClusterIP    None          <none>
   9090/TCP                               6h21m
pulsar-dev-zookeeper         ClusterIP    None          <none>
   8000/TCP,2888/TCP,3888/TCP,2181/TCP    6h21m
pulsar-dev-broker            ClusterIP    None          <none>
   8080/TCP,6650/TCP                      6h21m
```

pulsar-dev-grafana	LoadBalancer	10.43.58.168	172.19.0.2
3000:32186/TCP		6h21m	
pulsar-dev-pulsar-manager	LoadBalancer	10.43.65.36	172.19.0.2
9527:31150/TCP		6h21m	
pulsar-dev-proxy	LoadBalancer	10.43.98.79	172.19.0.2
80:30168/TCP,6650:31115/TCP		6h21m	

Pulsar Components

Now that a Kubernetes cluster with Pulsar is deployed, you want microservices to use the same. Inside a Kubernetes cluster, Pulsar clients can determine the broker location using Kubernetes service discovery. Pods running in a Kubernetes cluster are connected using DNS names. Each pod is configured with a service, having its own a fully qualified domain name in the format <serviceName>.<namespaceName>.svc.cluster.local. Clients can provide the full-service URL (pulsar-dev-broker.eventing.svc.cluster. local) and leave it to Kubernetes service discovery to resolve it to the correct broker address. If there are multiple brokers, Kubernetes automatically load balance requests among them. Moreover, the Pulser Helm chart deploys the following components for working with Apache Pulsar.

Pulsar Toolset

Pulsar toolset is an optional component for Apache Pulsar. It provides the set of command-line tools which are provided with the Apache Pulsar binary. You used these tools when developing solutions in the previous chapters. You can connect the toolset interactively using the following command.

```
$ kubectl exec -it -n eventing pulsar-dev-toolset-0 -- /bin/bash
```

Helm release has generated all required configurations for the deployed pulsar cluster. You can invoke commands like clusters/tenants/topics, as shown next, to interact with the cluster.

```
$ ./bin/pulsar-admin clusters list
"pulsar-dev"
```

Pulsar Proxy

Pulsar proxy is an optional component for Apache Pulsar (see Figure 8-1). Pulsar Publisher and subscribers often connect to the Pulsar broker directly. But in certain topologies, there is no direct access to the Pulsar broker, which is often deployed remotely to the Pulser client. Pulsar proxy is used in these scenarios to forward messages between the Pulsar client and the Pulsar broker, regardless of the topics to which messages are dispatched/ received. Thus, Pulsar proxy acts as a gateway to facilitate access to the deployed Pulsar broker.

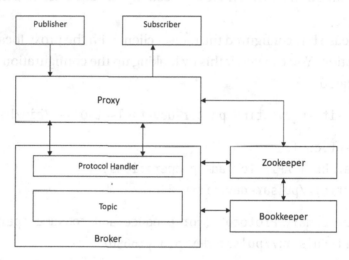

Figure 8-1. *Pulsar proxy*

Pulsar proxy is a stateless component that uses ZooKeeper to determine the location of brokers. It also monitors the status of each Pulsar broker. If a broker becomes unavailable or unreachable, the proxy route messages to a new Pulsar broker. For the sake of performance and fault tolerance, you can run as many instances of the Pulsar proxy as you'd like.

Pulsar proxy accesses the pulsar-admin REST API and the Pulsar binary protocol. It supports TLS encryption, thus facilitating the following topologies.

- TLS termination: Pulsar producer/subscribers enable TLS handshake with the proxy. On the other end, the proxy does a cleartext handshake with the broker.

- TLS end-to-end: Pulsar producer/subscribers enable TLS handshake with the proxy, and the proxy does a different TLS handshake with the broker.

For authorization needs, the proxy can also forward user credentials which the broker can validate. You can also enable the proxy protocol while configuring Pulsar proxy. By default, the Pulsar proxy forwards requests to the instances without modifying the request headers. Due to this, the broker cannot determine the source address for the request. The proxy protocol provides connection information from the source requesting the data to the destination for which the connection was requested in a human-readable header format.

The Helm release has configured the toolset client with the proxy location instead of the broker location. You can verify this by looking up the configuration that the Helm release has generated.

```
$ kubectl exec -it -n eventing pulsar-dev-toolset-0 -- /bin/bash
```

```
$ cat conf/client.conf
# URL for Pulsar REST API (for admin operations)
webServiceUrl=http://pulsar-dev-proxy:80/
```

```
# URL for Pulsar Binary Protocol (for produce and consume operations)
brokerServiceUrl=pulsar://pulsar-dev-proxy:6650/
```

All Apache Pulsar components are deployed within the eventing namespace. Thus they can resolve each other only service names instead of FQDN.

In the Kubernetes cluster, the proxy is exposed as a load balancer service, as shown in the previous section. Thus, it is reachable from external networks and can be used as follows.

```
$ ./bin/pulsar-admin  --admin-URL http://172.19.0.2/ tenants list
"public"
"pulsar"
```

Pulsar Manager

Pulsar Manager is an open source web console for managing Apache Pulsar. It can be used not only for operations aspects but also for monitoring statistics and broker information of the Pulsar cluster. A Pulsar Manager is capable of managing multiple Pulsar clusters. You can perform the following functions.

- Tenant management

- Namespaces management

- Topics management

- Subscriptions management

- Brokers management

- Clusters management

Pulsar Helm release also deploys Pulsar Manager with external access. You can open the manager console by accessing the associated service URL.

```
$ kubectl get svc pulsar-dev-pulsar-manager -n eventing
NAME                             TYPE           CLUSTER-IP     EXTERNAL-IP
    PORT(S)          AGE
pulsar-dev-pulsar-manager    LoadBalancer   10.43.65.36    172.19.0.2
    9527:31150/TCP    29h
```

The service runs on port 9527, so you can access it using http://172.19.0.2:9527/ (see Figure 8-2). The console would ask for a username and password. This is stored in Kubernetes secrets encoded in base64 format. You can retrieve the same using the command.

Figure 8-2. *Pulsar Manager*

```
$ kubectl get secrets pulsar-dev-pulsar-manager-secret -n eventing -o
jsonpath='{.data.PULSAR_MANAGER_ADMIN_USER}' | base64 --decode
pulsar
```

You can read the password using data.PULSAR_MANAGER_ADMIN_PASSWORD as JsonPath. You can access the console using the determined username and password. Pulsar Manager organizes a Pulsar instance or a group of Pulsar clusters as an environment. You can create an environment called dev and provide the broker URL as http://pulsar-dev-broker.eventing.svc.cluster.local:8080/.

Pulsar Manager would quickly discover the associated tenants, namespaces, topics, and message exchange rates. You can click the dev environment to list all these details.

Deployment

Now that the infrastructure is in place, you can deploy the microservice solution developed in Chapter 5. Previously you created a portfolio tracking solution consisting of server microservices.

The WizKap Inc. portfolio tracker solution has a portfolio service, which is responsible for aggregating the prices published by EquityPriceCalcutor and BondPriceCalculator (see Figure 8-3). These prices must be used to calculate valuations for every user.

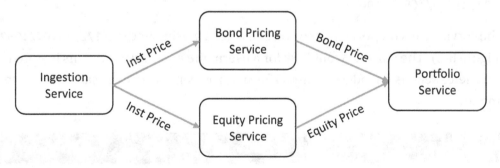

Figure 8-3. *Microservices*

Let's deploy the solution. There can be many topologies with multiple instances of each service. But for the sake of simplicity, you can do the following.

- Deploy the producer outside the Kubernetes cluster. It connects via the Pulsar proxy.

- Deploy the functions inside the Pulsar broker using the process runtime.

- Deploy the consumer inside the Kubernetes cluster. It connects directly to the Pulsar broker.

The following diagram (see Figure 8-4) shows the deployment topology.

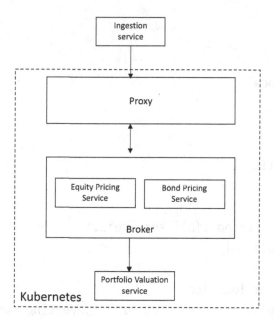

Figure 8-4. *Deployment topology*

First, you need to package the portfolio service as a Docker image, running the executable JAR. The executable should be provided with the location of the Pulsar broker.

```
FROM azul/zulu-openjdk:11
COPY target/PortfolioService-1.0-SNAPSHOT.jar portfolioService.jar
ENV pulsar_location "pulsar://localhost:6550/"
CMD ["java","-Xms1024m","-Xmx2048m", "-jar","/portfolioService.
jar",$pulsar_location]
```

You can deploy the service using the following YAML with the *kubectl* apply command. It is recommended to inject environment parameters using Kubernetes configmaps.

```
$ cat <<EOF | kubectl create -f -
apiVersion: apps/v1
kind: Deployment
metadata:
  name: portfoliocal
  labels:
    app: portfoliocal
spec:
  replicas: 1
  selector:
    matchLabels:
      app: portfoliocal
  template:
    metadata:
      labels:
        app: portfoliocal
    spec:
      containers:
      - image: rahul0208/portfolioservice:1.1
        name: portfoliocal
        env:
        - name: pulsar_location
          value: "pulsar://pulsar-dev-broker.eventing.svc.cluster.
          local:6650/"
EOF
```

Next, you need to deploy the functions using the pulsar-admin command. The command must specify the admin-URL which is the HTTP URL of Pulsar proxy. Invoke the. following command to deploy both functions.

```
./bin/pulsar-admin --admin-url http://172.19.0.2/ functions create --jar
priceCalculator/target/PriceCalculator-1.0-SNAPSHOT-jar-with-dependencies.
jar --classname EquityPriceCalculator --name eq-calculator  --inputs day-
end-price  --schema-type json --output eq-day-end-price
```

```
./bin/pulsar-admin --admin-url http://172.19.0.2/ functions create --jar
priceCalculator/target/PriceCalculator-1.0-SNAPSHOT-jar-with-dependencies.
jar --classname BondPriceCalculator --name bond-calculator  --inputs day-
end-price  --schema-type json --output bond-day-end-price
```

You can run the ingestion service as an executable JAR. The service must connect to the Pulsar proxy using pulsar protocol on port 6650. There is no change for this service, except the location of Pulsar.

```
void initialize() throws PulsarClientException {
      client = PulsarClient.builder()
             .serviceUrl("pulsar://172.19.0.2:6650")
             .build();

      dayEndPriceProducer = client.newProducer(JSONSchema.
      of(InstrumentClosePrice.class))
             .topic("day-end-price")
             .create();
  }
```

Once the ingestion service is started, it would push valuations for various stocks, which are computed by the consumer deployed inside the Kubernetes cluster. You can use the kubectl logs command to verify the processing.

Pulsar Storage

Pulsar Helm deployment provides many options for storage. In Kubernetes clusters, the local disk is temporary and can't be trusted for permanent storage. Alternatively, Kubernetes provides persistent volumes for permanent storage in the cluster.

To use the persistent volume, let's create a cluster on AWS-managed Kubernetes service, EKS. You can't use this on the local variants of the Kubernetes as they lack a volume provisioner. As stated before, there is no change in steps for installing Pulsar on managed Kubernetes. The differences are in Helm values, where you enable persistence. You are going to deploy Pulsar on a Kubernetes cluster consisting of two large worker nodes.

```
$ helm install    --set initialize=true  --set affinity.anti_affinity=false
--namespace eventing  pulsar-dev apache/pulsar
NAME: pulsar-dev
LAST DEPLOYED: Thu Sep 16 23:02:33 2021
NAMESPACE: eventing
STATUS: deployed
REVISION: 1
TEST SUITE: None
```

This command has not supplied a value.yml file. Thus the Helm command applies the default configurations, which has persistence enabled along with multiple instances of each component.

It is important to note that you configured anti-affinity by supplying affinity.anti_affinity=false in the preceding command. The flag makes sure that multiple instances of a component are deployed on different Kubernetes worker nodes. If the flag is not passed, you need at least four node clusters as there are four instances of BookKeeper. The flag has been passed to keep the cluster hardware requirement low.

Next, let's determine which persistent volumes have been added by the release. This is done by using the following command.

```
$ kubectl get pv -n eventing
NAME                                        CAPACITY    ACCESS
MODES    RECLAIM POLICY    STATUS    CLAIM
STORAGECLASS    REASON    AGE
pvc-199bdee6-bb39-4e55-8f87-b92df83068f2    50Gi
RWO           Delete             Bound     eventing/pulsar-dev-bookie-
ledgers-pulsar-dev-bookie-0      gp2                       138m
pvc-324c5a86-e313-4b92-a51e-76e60dda836b    20Gi        RWO            Delete
Bound     eventing/pulsar-dev-zookeeper-data-pulsar-dev-
zookeeper-0    gp2                       138m
pvc-3758fc56-f2f0-419f-972e-82e8ba44b9ea    10Gi
RWO           Delete             Bound     eventing/pulsar-dev-bookie-
journal-pulsar-dev-bookie-1      gp2                       138m
```

CHAPTER 8　DEPLOYING PULSAR ON KUBERNETES

```
pvc-58e641f4-ce30-4c72-97b8-9bfa8c1befe9    50Gi
RWO            Delete           Bound      eventing/pulsar-dev-bookie-
ledgers-pulsar-dev-bookie-1       gp2                    138m
pvc-60ee8247-e5d7-40b5-a5ae-d3a4b9cf74d1   20Gi       RWO              Delete
Bound    eventing/pulsar-dev-zookeeper-data-pulsar-dev-
zookeeper-2   gp2                    101s
pvc-cdf5fd73-757c-48db-96a2-876637eed258   20Gi       RWO              Delete
Bound    eventing/pulsar-dev-zookeeper-data-pulsar-dev-
zookeeper-1   gp2                    137m
pvc-f0d27f1c-0cc2-4340-88bf-fe277ec7c589    10Gi
RWO            Delete           Bound      eventing/pulsar-dev-bookie-
journal-pulsar-dev-bookie-0       gp2                    138m
```

You can see that the default configuration created the following three types of volumes.

- **data**: the volume is 20 GB, used by ZooKeeper

- **ledger**: the volume is 50 GB, used by BookKeeper

- **journal**: the volume is 10 GB, used by BookKeeper

Kubernetes provides you the flexibility to modify the size of these volumes dynamically. You can change the size of these volumes using the following configuration in the Helm release custom-values.yml.

```
zookeeper:
volumes:
  persistence: true
  data:
      name: data
      size: 5Gi
      storageClassName: gp2
      local_storage: false
bookkeeper:
  volumes:
    persistence: true
    journal:
      name: journal
```

```
      size: 5Gi
      local_storage: false
      storageClassName: gp2
    ledgers:
      name: ledgers
      size: 5Gi
      local_storage: false
```

Next, upgrade the release using the following command.

```
$ helm upgrade  --values custom.yaml    --set affinity.anti_affinity=false
--namespace eventing  pulsar-dev apache/pulsar
```

You can verify that the size has changed for all volumes to 5 GB. This configuration used a general-purpose disk, specified by gp2. You can use any other type of supported volume as well. There are parameters to define custom type as well. The configuration also shows a local_storage option, a special type of persistent storage attached to the Kubernetes cluster.

Tiered Storage

Apache Pulsar uses a segment-oriented architecture to store topics. Topics in Pulsar are persisted to an Apache BookKeeper managed ledger, also known as a managed log. The log consists of an ordered list of segments (see Figure 8-5). Due to the append-only architecture of a log, Pulsar only writes to the final segment. Segments previous to the current one are sealed, and their data becomes effectively immutable.

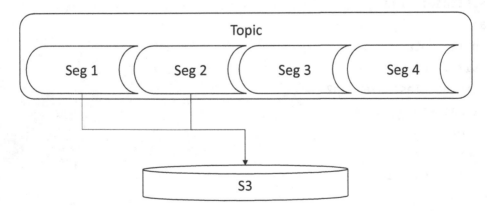

Figure 8-5. *Segmentation*

Tiered storage offloading leverages this segment-oriented architecture. Offloading segments to an external storage system involves copying the log segments to the external storage system. You can offload all segments of the log, other than the segment currently being written to.

Here again, the AWS EKS Pulsar cluster configures tiered storage. You should be able to do this with a multi-node local cluster. The first step is to create an S3 bucket used as tiered storage (see Figure 8-6). This is done using the following steps.

1. Log in to the AWS console.

2. Choose the S3 service.

3. Click the Create Bucket button.

4. On the form, provide a bucket name.

5. Uncheck "Block all public access".

6. Click the Create button to get the S3 bucket.

Figure 8-6. *S3 bucket*

Configure

To use tiered storage, you must enable the AWS S3 offloader driver. This is accomplished by specifying the relevant configuration options in the broker. You would need the following details.

- Bucket Name determines the AWS S3 bucket, specified as managedLedgerOffloadDriver.

- Bucket Region is the AWS region where a bucket is located. It is specified as s3ManagedLedgerOffloadRegion.

- AWS access credentials, specified as Java system properties aws. accessKeyId and aws.secretKey to PULSAR_EXTRA_OPTS.

Specify these values in the Helm custom-values.yaml under broker.configData.

```
broker:
  component: broker
  replicaCount: 2
  configData:
    managedLedgerOffloadDriver : "aws-s3"
    s3ManagedLedgerOffloadRegion : "us-east-1"
    s3ManagedLedgerOffloadBucket : "pulsar-tiered-storage-2"
    PULSAR_EXTRA_OPTS: "-Daws.accessKeyId=XXXXXXXXX -Daws.secretKey=
    XXXXXXXXX-XXXXXXXXX"
    managedLedgerMaxEntriesPerLedger: "500"
    managedLedgerMinLedgerRolloverTimeMinutes: "1"
```

You change the ledger size and rollover time for this setup to make topics create each segment more easily. These values are responsible for doing ledger rollover at shorter intervals. Their default values are recommended for the production environment. To make these changes effective, you must upgrade the Helm release using the following command.

```
$ helm upgrade  --values custom.yaml    --set affinity.anti_affinity=false
--namespace eventing  pulsar-dev apache/pulsar
```

Note   The current helm chart does not support the tiered storage configuration beyond AWS. The work is in progress, and future versions include support for Google Cloud and Microsoft Azure.

Offloading

Segment offloading is the process of transferring messages to S3. You can trigger it manually as well as automatically based on some threshold. But before you can offload messages, you must generate a few messages using the following command.

```
$ kubectl exec -it -n eventing pulsar-dev-toolset-0 -- /bin/bash
```

```
$./bin/pulsar-client produce test-pulsar-offload --messages
"Produce  Messages for Offloeading" --rate 0 --num-produce 1000
```

In a different terminal tab, run the consume command to make sure topic data is not dropped.

```
$ kubectl exec -it -n eventing pulsar-dev-toolset-0 -- /bin/bash
$ ./bin/pulsar-client consume -s "read-data" test-pulsar-offload
```

Next, you can trigger an AWS S3 offloader manually using the CLI. You need to specify the maximum amount of data (threshold) retained on a Pulsar cluster for a topic. If the size of the topic data on the Pulsar cluster exceeds this threshold, segments from the topic are moved to AWS S3 until the threshold is no longer exceeded. Older segments are moved first.

```
$ kubectl exec -it -n eventing pulsar-dev-toolset-0 -- /bin/bash
$./bin/pulsar topics offload  test-pulsar-offload -s 100
Offload triggered for persistent://public/default/test-pulsar-offload for
messages before 6:0:-1
```

You can check the status of offload process using the following command.

```
$ kubectl exec -it -n eventing pulsar-dev-toolset-0 -- /bin/bash
$ ./bin/pulsar-admin topics offload-status persistent://public/default/
test-pulsar-offload
```

Once the status is "success," you can find the offloaded ledger in S3 using the AWS console. Executing offloading process manually is a cumbersome task. The Pulsar also supports automatic offloading using namespace policies. The policy can be configured to offload data automatically once a threshold is reached. The threshold is based on the data size that a topic has stored on a Pulsar cluster (see Table 8-1). Once the topic reaches the threshold, an offloading operation is triggered automatically.

Table 8-1. *Offloading trigger*

Threshold value	Action
> 0	Triggers the offloading operation
= 0	Causes a broker to offload data as soon as possible
< 0	Disables automatic offloading operation

Automatic offloading runs when a new segment is added to a topic log. If you set the threshold on a namespace, but few messages are being produced to the topic, offload does not work until the current segment is full. You can set the AWS S3 offloader threshold size using the following command.

```
$ kubectl exec -it -n eventing pulsar-dev-toolset-0 -- /bin/bash
$ ./bin/pulsar-admin namespaces set-offload-threshold --size 10M default/
test-pulsar-offload
```

Pulsar Geo-replication

Geo-replication offers a disaster recovery solution to prevent data loss in a regional disaster or a large-scale outage. Application failover can be initiated to a secondary Pulsar cluster if geo-replication is enabled. Besides disaster recovery, geo-replication often supports edge computing, where each cluster is responsible for all business applications while keeping data in sync between them.

Active geo-replication in Apache Pulsar allows you to create readable secondary Pulsar clusters in the same or different data center. As a prerequisite, you would need two clusters. Please create them as outlined in the Installation section. Let's name them pulsar-a and pulsar-b, respectively. Then add the cluster pulser-b in pulsar-a and vice-versa using the following command.

```
$ kubectl exec -it pod/pulsar-a-toolset-0 -n eventing bash
$ bin/pulsar-admin clusters create \
  --broker-url pulsar://192.168.1.6:6650 \
```

```
  --url http://192.168.1.6:80 \
  pulsar-b

$ kubectl exec -it pod/pulsar-b-toolset-0 -n eventing bash
$ bin/pulsar-admin clusters create \
  --broker-url pulsar://192.168.1.5:6650 \
  --url http://192.168.1.5:80 \
  pulsar-a
```

Pulsar allows configuring geo-replication on tenants. Only tenants with access to both clusters can enable geo-replication between them. Namespace policies provide access to both tenants. Messages published in a namespace also be replicated to all the other clusters. Thus, you must create a tenant in both clusters and configure it for both clusters.

```
$ kubectl exec -it pod/pulsar-b-toolset-0 -n eventing bash
$ bin/pulsar-admin tenants create replicated-tenant \
  --admin-roles my-admin-role \
  --allowed-clusters    pulsar-a,pulsar-b
```

Next you must create the namespace in both clusters and configure it for both clusters.

```
$ kubectl exec -it pod/pulsar-b-toolset-0 -n eventing bash
$ bin/pulsar-admin namespaces create replicated-tenant/ replicated-namespace
$ bin/pulsar-admin namespaces set-clusters replicated-tenant/ replicated
-namespace --clusters pulsar-a,pulsar-b
```

That's it. You have enabled full replication across clusters pulsar-a and pulsar-b. You can produce messages in pulsar-a and consumer then in pulsar-b.

```
$ kubectl exec -it pod/pulsar-b-toolset-0 -n eventing bash
$ bin/pulsar-client consume replicated-tenant/replicated-namespace/
plaintext -s "text-subscription" -n 0

$ kubectl exec -it pod/pulsar-a-toolset-0 -n eventing bash
$ bin/pulsar-client produce replicated-tenant/replicated-namespace/
plaintext --messages "AttackAtOnce"
```

This discussion enabled a full-duplex replication where messages in one cluster are actively synched in the second cluster. The following topologies are also available.

- **Active-Passive**: This is a one-way replication where messages from the active cluster are synced in the passive cluster. The passible cluster becomes active in case of failure of the primary cluster.

- **Aggregated**: This is again a one-way replication where messages from an active cluster are synced in the aggregated cluster. Unlike the active-passive topology, there are multiple active clusters. The aggregated cluster is responsible for receiving messages from multiple Pulsar clusters, aggregating them in some manner, and then performing some active business processing.

Pulsar Monitoring

A Pulsar cluster can handle a significant amount of data. It's important to monitor the health of your Apache Pulsar deployment to maintain reliable performance for the applications that depend on it since Apache Pulsar consists of several components, so it generates metrics at several levels.

- Zookeeper metrics

- Broker metrics

- Functions matrixes

- BookKeeper metrics

- Proxy metrics

- Producer metrics

- Consumer metrics

In Pulsar, brokers are responsible for all message exchanges, so monitoring and alerting on issues as they emerge in the broker cluster is critical. There are several attributes, but the attributes described in the following sections are useful in tracking performance and raising alerts.

pulsar_function_process_latency_ms

The metric measures the total time is taken to service a request by a function. It includes time taken to ack/nack the message as well as to perform any processing. There is also a 1min variant that captures the latency of the last executed function process. The value should be quite small, with most of the time taken at the message processing. Large values must indicate optimizations in the created function logic.

pulsar_storage_write_latency_le

It captures storage throughput for the messages in a namespace or a topic. The data is of significance if durability is enabled in synchronous mode. Tracking latency at storage level s gives you more information as to how bookies are performing.

bookie_journal_JOURNAL_SYNC

Pulsar controls local durability by writing or fsyncing data to a journal disk(s). It controls whether a bookie fsyncs data to journal disks before returning a written acknowledgment to brokers. The system returns a write response to the peer/client ONLY AFTER the data has been successfully fsynced to local disks (local durability) or replicated to multiple locations (replication durability). The metric provides a summary of the latency of syncing data to the journal disk.

pulsar_source_written_total / pulsar_sink_written_total

You should monitor the rate of requests from your producers, consumers, and followers to ensure Pulsar is communicating efficiently. You can expect the Pulsar request rate to rise as producers send more traffic or the deployment scales out, adding consumers or followers that need to fetch messages. But if throughput remains high, you should consider increasing the batch size on the producers, consumers, and/or brokers. This can improve the throughput of Pulsar deployment by reducing the number of requests, thereby decreasing unnecessary network overhead.

pulsar_ml_NumberOfMessagesInBacklog

The number of backlog messages for all the consumers. In a queue-based system, when processing stops but messages keep arriving, the message debt can accumulate a large backlog, which will drive up the processing time. Work can be completed too late for the results to be useful, essentially causing the availability hit that queueing was meant to guard against.

pulsar_storage_size

A broker owns the total size of the topics of this namespace. As Pulsar persists all data to disk, monitoring the amount of free disk space available is necessary. It is very important that you keep track of disk growth over time and set alerts to inform administrators at an appropriate amount of time before disk space is all but used up.

pulsar_replication_backlog

A replication backlog is the number of messages produced to the origin cluster but not yet replicated to the other remote clusters. Keeping track of the replication backlog is crucial for two reasons.

- If the origin cluster fails over to the destination cluster, all messages produced at the origin and haven't yet reached the destination are inaccessible until the origin data center goes online again.

- The backlog delays any message processing that happens at the destination.

The backlog is typically just a few messages, but it can grow larger if the network partitions. If the backlog keeps growing, the replication throughput is lower than what is being produced at the origin cluster.

Monitoring Dashboard

Pulsar Helm release also deploys monitoring stack inclusive of Prometheus, Alert-manager, and Grafana. Prometheus is a tool used for aggregating multiple platform metrics while scraping hundreds of endpoints. It is purpose-built for scrape and aggregation use cases. Internally, it contains a time-series data store that allows you to store and retrieve time-sliced data in an optimized fashion. Grafana is an open source charting and dashboarding tool that talks to Prometheus and renders beautiful graphs. In the following section, you build a monitoring chart using the Grafana dashboard.

The Pulsar Helm release also provides options for configuring Prometheus and Grafana. The Helm chart provides the following default values. If you have already deployed these components to observe other applications, you can turn down the flags and use the same infrastructure to monitor Pulsar components.

```
monitoring:
  # monitoring - prometheus
  prometheus: true
  # monitoring - grafana
  grafana: true
  # monitoring - node_exporter
  node_exporter: true
  # alerting - alert-manager
  alert_manager: true
```

You can verify these components by looking up the exposed services.

```
$ kubectl get svc pulsar-dev-grafana -n eventing
NAME                    TYPE          CLUSTER-IP      EXTERNAL-IP
   PORT(S)          AGE
pulsar- dev -grafana    LoadBalancer  10.43.58.168    172.19.0.2
   3000:32186/TCP    2d3h
```

You can access the Grafana dashboard from http://172.19.0.2:3000/ (see Figure 8-7). It would require a username and password, both of which are part of Kubernetes secrets.

```
$ kubectl get secrets pulsar-dev-grafana-secret -n pulsar -o jsonpath='{.
data.GRAFANA_ADMIN_PASSWORD}' | base64 --decode
pulsar
```

Figure 8-7. *Grafana login*

Rather than building new Grafana dashboards from scratch, you can import them from Grafana's marketplace, which hosts community-created dashboards. Add a dashboard by navigating to Dashboards ➤ Manage by clicking the four-square icon on the left navigation bar (see Figure 8-8). You can find the broker dashboard in the list of available dashboards.

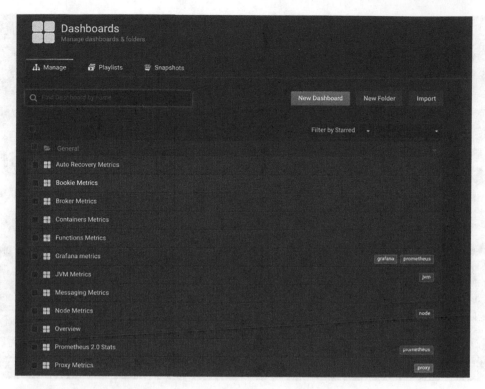

Figure 8-8. *Grafana dashboard*

Once you click the broker metrics, it opens the required dashboard, along with its monitoring charts. The chart has been configured on the Prometheus data source. You can shuffle through the different tenants/namespaces to get their respective monitoring information (see Figure 8-9). The list also contains several other dashboards, such as JVM, Node, Proxy, and Bookics. Once the dashboard is clicked, it becomes part of the Grafana landing home page.

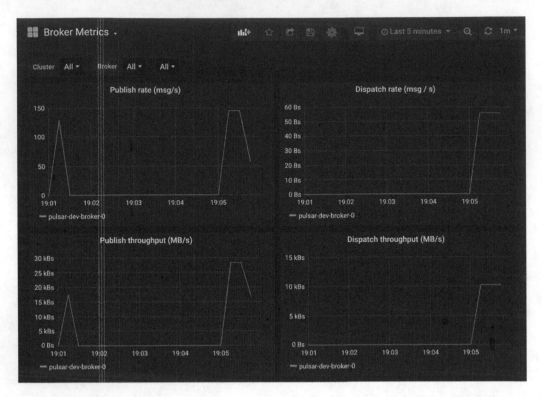

Figure 8-9. *Broker charts*

Summary

This chapter explained how to deploy and configure Pulsar on top of Kubernetes using its Helm chart. You looked at the various storage options. You also worked with the Kubernetes monitoring stack to monitor Pulsar metrics. With that, you come to the end of this chapter and this book.

Pulsar is rapidly evolving, and we encourage you to head over to Pulsar's official documentation to continue your exploratory journey of Apache Pulsar.

Index

© Rahul Sharma and Mohammad Atyab 2022
R. Sharma and M. Atyab, *Cloud-Native Microservices with Apache Pulsar*,
https://doi.org/10.1007/978-1-4842-7839-0

Printed in the United States by Baker & Taylor Publisher Services

Printed in the United States
by Baker & Taylor Publisher Services